QUÉBEC INC.
and the temptation of State Capitalism

Canadian Cataloguing in Publication Data

Arbour, Pierre, 1935-

Quebec Inc. and the temptation of state capitalism

Translation of: Québec inc. et la tentation du dirigisme.

ISBN 1-895854-14-8

1. Public investments - Quebec (Province).   2. Caisse de dépôt et place-ment du Québec.   3. Quebec (Province) - Economic policy.   4. Corpora-tions, Government - Quebec (Province).   5. Government business enterprises - Quebec (Province).   I. Title

HC117.Q4A7213 1993   332.6'7252'09714   C94-940026-2

If you would like to be kept informed of our forthcoming
publications, please send your request to :
Robert Davies Publishing, P.O. Box 702, Outremont, QC H2V 4N6

Pierre Arbour

QUÉBEC INC.
and the temptation of State Capitalism

translated by
Madeleine Hébert

ROBERT DAVIES PUBLISHING
MONTREAL—TORONTO

Distributed in Canada by

Stewart House,
380 Esna Park Drive
Markham, ON L3R 1H5

☎ (Ontario & Quebec)1-800-268-5707
☎ (Rest of Canada) 1-800-268-5742

FAX 1-905-940-8864

Original title:

Québec Inc. et la tentation du dirigisme

The publisher gratefully acknowledges the support of the
Canada Council for the translation of this book.
Copyright © 1993 Robert Davies Publishing,
a division of l'Étincelle éditeur inc.

ISBN 1-895854-14-8
2   3   4   5   93   94

For my daughter Christine,
and my wife Chantal,
whose support was precious

Table of Contents

CHAPTER SIX
Quebec Inc. and linguistic interventionism 160

List of Tables

PREFACE

AFTER HAVING MANAGED the stock portfolio of the Caisse de Dépôt et Placement and having made its first investment in stocks at the beginning of 1967, I enjoyed many fruitful years at the Caisse under the presidency of Claude Prieur, who unfortunately died suddenly in 1973. I also worked for several years under the presidency of Marcel Cazavan, previously a Quebec Deputy Minister of Finance. Mr. Cazavan initiated the policy of a closer relationship between the Caisse and the provincial government, especially from 1977 on, the time when Jacques Parizeau became the new Finance Minister following the election of the Parti Québécois.

In 1976, I was given the responsibility of acting in company mergers as Senior Corporate Investment Advisor at the Caisse de Dépôt. I was instrumental in the purchase of M. Loeb by Provigo in 1978 and the subsequent merger of its Edmonton subsidiary Horne & Pitfield with Market Wholesale of California. Finally, I was also active in many complex and sensitive dossiers such as Gaz Métropolitain-Norcen, Québecair, Asbestos Corporation and Campeau Corporation.

In May 1979, I felt the time was right for me to switch from the Caisse de Dépôt to the private sector. I created my own business specializing in oil investments, Alkebec Inc., with the help of Pierre Mercier, a former analyst at the Caisse. I was far from expecting the political upheavals that would hit the Caisse a few months later in January 1980 when Jean Campeau was unexpectedly nominated as its head. This nomination would result in the resignations of all the portfolio managers of the Caisse and of almost all the assistant managers and analysts of the stock portfolios.

Over the course of the years, I was able to observe the growing importance of the Caisse in the economy of the province of Quebec due to the influx of the millions of dollars it invested. I could also see that, starting mainly in 1978, the political power structure had an important presence at the Caisse and that investment decisions were often dictated by political priorities.

In the course of my research for this book, I also read a book published in 1989 titled *La Machine à milliards (The Billion-Dollar Machine*, never released in English) by Mario Pelletier that relates the history of the Caisse de Dépôt et Placement du Québec. In that book, the author quotes part of a letter addressed to the President of the Caisse, written in 1978 by André Marier, a new Caisse director and the political representative of Quebec premier René Lévesque : "Up to now, the successful transactions (such as Provigo-Loeb and National Cablevision for example) seem to me so few that I have to ask myself if the Caisse does not have a deliberate strategy of dispersing its investments as much as possible so as to make its presence as discrete as possible. By acting this way, we will never be able to fundamentally modify the industrial structure of Quebec."

The two investments referred to by André Marier eventually generated massive gains for the Caisse. By 1979, the value of the Caisse's initial investment in Provigo had quadrupled, from $6 million to $24 million. As for National Cablevision, the small investment made in 1971 in the amount of $3.2 million in what was then a small company would eventually be valued in the vicinity of $100 million as that company evolved into the Vidéotron media giant.

Immediately after this letter was written, in 1980, the new administration of the Caisse enthusiastically adopted a course of action proposed by André Marier — and probably inspired by Bernard Landry, a Minister in the Lévesque cabinet. In a September 1978 interview with the Quebec City newspaper *Le Soleil*, Mr. Landry "is taking into consideration the possibility of creating an agency able to use the Caisse money in a more dynamic and more direct way". But the government did not have to create that new agency after all, because as it turned out, the new administration at the Caisse de Dépôt was about to make its own presence felt in a massive way, leaving far behind the two initial intvestments quoted by André Marier whose total cost was less than $10 million of Caisse funds.

Encouraged by my publisher, I decided to put down on paper my thoughts regarding the general, and vast, subject of the impact of state agencies, provincial as well as municipal, in Quebec's economy. These agencies drain an important part of our financial resources, and the citizenry, ill-informed at best, has been unable to react to this economic fact. I have spent long hours analyzing the annual reports and the press releases of our large Quebec state corporations and I interviewed many people who played a role in what is obviously our own Quebec brand of state capitalism. Relying also on my own recollections, I was able to reconstruct the major events and analyze their consequences.

My main motivation for writing this book was to warn the coming generation of the dangers of unchecked state capitalism and to show the consequences of thirty years of state intervention. It is not without some apprehension that I take this public stand, because I am aware that by throwing this rather large rock into Quebec's small millpond, I may be providing ammunition to some who wish Quebec ill, who may try to maliciously tarnish Quebec's image outside the province, even if other provinces and other governments have been guilty of as bad or even worse. The financial disasters of BRIC in British Columbia, NOVATEL in Alberta, UTDC in Ontario and SYSCO in Nova Scotia should be etched on our collective memories, in this respect.

Still, I consider it very important that the population know what has been done at the Caisse de Dépôt, particularly under the direction of Jean Campeau. As for Jacques Parizeau, who was able to win over a succession of Quebec's premiers to his ideas using a mixture of eloquence and intelligence, he is the one who must ultimately take responsibility for most of the policies of the Caisse de Dépôt and the state corporations described in this book.

Whenever the question of investing our pension funds comes up, I must say that there is a common thread running through the actions of our elected officials and of high state officials — the sincere desire to increase the collective wealth by spectacular investments. This attitude perhaps stems from a desire to compensate for French Canadians' historical lack of economic power, power that used to be the exclusive preserve of the Anglophones. Unconsciously, perhaps we all wanted to emulate men like Paul Desmarais, the President of Power Corporation, but success has been unfortunately in sparing supply. The worst aspect of the situation is that the real losers are not the rich, not the anonymous private investors of the market, but rather the whole population of Quebec, passive and captive to events decided without their approval and often without their ken. All Quebecers, as unwilling shareholders, emerged poorer from these adventures.

I thought it was appropriate in this book to evaluate the different subsidy programs offered by the government and also the most popular tax loopholes, in order to reflect on their respective merits.

Drawing on my experience as an administrator in both small and large companies, I also talk about some capitalist and bureaucratic abuses to which our society should give a long critical look.

Finally I give my reflections on another kind of state intervention, the linguistic laws whose constraining clutch is, together with high taxation, partially responsible for the relative impoverishment of Quebec at a time when we are at critical stage of our development as a francophone community.

CHAPTER 1

La Caisse De Dépôt et Placement Du Québec

DURING THE SEVENTIES, the world was stunned by the spectacular and successful ascension of the Japanese economy. Rebounding quickly after the Second World War, the result of a partnership between the Economics ministry, banks and industrialists, this constellation of forces became known as Japan Inc. During the last decade, some of Quebec's journalists found a parallel between that Japanese situation and the efforts that were being made in Quebec during the time immediately following the so-called Quiet Revolution. Because of this apparent parallel, the term "Québec Inc." was coined and rapidly caught on.

The avowed goal of the policies described by that expression was to try to create in Quebec the same kind of partnership between some of our most dynamic industrialists, the different provincial ministries dealing with the economy and the large state corporations, principally the Caisse de Dépôt et Placement du Québec.

THE CAISSE DE DÉPÔT ET PLACEMENT: PROFILE AND GOALS

"Created in 1965 by a law of Quebec's National Assembly, the Caisse de Dépôt et Placement, as a fund manager, invests money from pension funds, retirement insurance plans and various other public agencies. Its main goals are to obtain maximum financial return and to contribute by its actions to the dynamism of Quebec's economy while maintaining the security of the funds under its control. The Caisse — whose head offices are located in Montreal, still an important financial centre — is one of the biggest institutions of its kind in North America and the premier fund manager in Canada in terms of invested capital."[1]

This institution began operations on January 1, 1966, in order to invest contributions from the Quebec Pension Board into market instruments such as stocks, bonds and real estate, as opposed to the Canada Pension Plan which invests its fund by lending it back to the provinces and is given a return on contributions based on ten-year maturity Government of Canada bonds. This original Quebec approach has resulted in a better return to the Caisse de Dépôt depositors than what the Canada Pension Plan

---

1   Annual Report 1992, Caisse de Dépôt et Placement du Québec.

obtained for its own depositors, in spite of the events and policies described in this book.

"I can say to you that, in the minds of its founders, it (the Caisse de Dépôt et Placement du Québec) was to perform much more than the simple efficient management of the funds on deposit, being also a conscious mechanism for transforming the industrial structures of Quebec on a long term basis."[2]

"The mandate of the Société de développement industriel (Industrial Development Corporation) was always to stimulate the economic development of Quebec. Principal financial arm of Quebec's governments for their economic policies, the corporation helped to develop and modernize a large part of the province's industrial structure."[3]

On the one hand here, we have in the first paragraph of this section the goals of the Caisse de Dépôt as defined in its 1992 annual report which are on much the same lines as its initial mandate established by its directors in 1966; on the other hand we have a new and somewhat different mandate as

2   Letter addressed to Marcel Cazavan (then President and director of the Caisse de Dépôt) by André Marier (adviser to premier René Lévesque and administrator of the Caisse de Dépôt), March 17, 1978.
3   Annual Report 1991-1992, *Société de développement industriel du Québec.*

quoted in André Marier's letter of March 17, 1978 and which was imposed by the political power structure after the nomination of Jean Campeau as the President of the Caisse in 1980. Finally, we have the goals of the *Société de développement industriel* as defined in its annual report, that actually look a lot like those that were pursued by the Caisse de Dépôt between 1980 and 1990. What happened during those years was actually a major confusion of objectives between these two state agencies, a confusion which led to the kind of results we propose to analyze later in this book.

MY CAREER AT THE CAISSE

Sometime in the middle of the winter of 1963 (the exact date is no longer clear and in any event not that important), I first met Jacques Parizeau, who was then a lecturer at the École des hautes études commerciales (H.E.C.) in Montreal. At that time, I was working as a financial analyst on Saint-James street, formerly the financial district of Montreal. During the course of an animated discussion about the difficulty Quebec had in selling its bonds in the rest of the country, he asked me if I would keep him informed about what I learned concerning the financing of the public debt of the Province of Quebec and of Hydro-Québec.

Jacques Parizeau was also a special adviser to the Lesage government, a man who had used his talents of persuasion during the nationalization of the electric utility companies located in Quebec in 1962, nationalization which created Hydro-Québec. During the spring of 1964, Mr. Parizeau told me in confidence that "big projects" were being prepared in Quebec City and that the creation of a state agency modelled after the French *Caisse des dépôts et consignations* was being contemplated in order to manage the *Régie des Rentes du Québec* or R.R.Q. — Quebec's pension fund. He asked me to send him my ideas on the subject.

At that moment in the history of the province of Quebec, there was a kind of renewed social infatuation, a general trend if you will, best described as a love of everything French. Policy concepts of economic planning *à la française* were all the rage in Quebec City, and the idea of a future Caisse de Dépôt et Placement du Québec fitted very neatly into Jacques Parizeau's global conception of the value of economic planning. After a successful state harnessing of Quebec's hydro-electric resources with the nationalization of 1962,[4] the time had come to har-

---

4 Using a proven method in capitalist economies — i.e. purchasing more than 90% of the shares of the electric utility companies —, Quebec's government pulled off a remarkable coup without having to expropriate (as was discovered by the British-Columbia government a few years earlier, expropriation can be a risky business, often leading to lengthy and expensive litigation). By acquiring the electric utility companies via the route of direct offers to the shareholders, Hydro-Québec saved a great deal of money compared to the potential cost of expropriation followed by nationalization.

ness Quebecers' savings with the creation of the Caisse de Dépôt et de placement.

In 1965, Bill 51 creating the Caisse de Dépôt was adopted by the Liberal government of Jean Lesage. This law aimed to guarantee independence to the agency by providing a special status for its director, who was named to a ten year term and who could be removed only by a vote of the National Assembly.

During the summer of 1966, Claude Prieur, the new General Director of the Caisse de Dépôt, asked me to meet him to discuss the possibility of my being hired to take charge of the variable income portfolio. Having worked five years for an investment broker, the challenge was a significant one for me. I accepted his offer and started working at the Caisse on November 1st, 1966.

The first President of the Caisse de Dépôt came from the private sector, having worked in investments at the Sun Life Insurance Company for more than twenty years. He was highly qualified to manage this new institution that would gradually make its mark on the Canadian financial markets.

It was a great loss for us all when this dynamic man died suddenly from a stroke in April 1973. The assets of the Caisse at that time were $2.3 billion.

There were many months of delay during which the Caisse executive officers were hoping for the nomination of a new President with a background in the private sector similar to that of Claude Prieur. Finally, they learned that a career bureaucrat by the name of Marcel Cazavan was to become the new

President and General Manager of the Caisse. Mr. Cazavan had worked previously in Quebec City, particularly as Deputy Minister of Finance.

This ex-bureaucrat had job experience limited to the bond market (with a stockbroker prior to his employment at the Finance ministry in Quebec City) and never really understood the importance of having a large part of the Caisse assets in stocks. Even if the Caisse was constrained by its own rules to a cap of 30% ownership of any one company's shares held by the stock portfolio, it was impossible during the time when I was responsible for that portfolio under the presidency of Marcel Cazavan to go beyond a 15% asset commitment.

In 1977, I recall attending an investment meeting during which a discussion took place concerning the comparative yields on investments in stocks or bonds. The consensus was that long term returns on common shares were higher than bond returns. The Caisse's President, Mr. Cazavan, was not swayed by these arguments and adopted instead a rather paternalistic attitude on this issue. He recommended a larger, not smaller involvement of the agency in the bond market because of the possibility of obtaining in this way significant tax-free yields with fewer risks.

At the end of 1977, the percentage of stocks in the Caisse de Dépôt portfolio had sunk to only 13% after having reached 19.4% in 1973 during the presidency of Claude Prieur. But starting in 1980 under the new administration of Jean Campeau, the proportion of stocks in the Caisse portfolio increased considerably, and by 1991, it stood at more than 37%! Some might see this as having been one of the more positive aspects of the administration of Jean Campeau. But clearly, the point must also be made, and we will return to this later on, than when Caisse executives were in a position to act freely, with no political interference, they were able to carry off brilliant manoeuvers, for example when they bought 30% of the shares of Télésystème National for $2 million in 1984. In 1988, these shares alone were worth more than $40 million. Another example: in 1973, during the Claude Prieur administration, $1 300,000 was invested in Nordic Labs shares; the shares were sold in 1991 to Marion, Merill, Dow for approximately $65 million.

Finally, Marcel Cazavan wanted to enhance asset security and approved in 1976 a new way of managing the stock portfolio by weighting the portfolio using the Toronto Stock Exchange indexes. This extremely cautious attitude would allow André Marier (one of the most influential advisers to Jacques Parizeau) to push ahead with his own agenda after being named on the board of directors of the Caisse at the beginning of 1978.

André Marier was a career bureaucrat who had participated in 1964 in the elaboration of the initial project for the creation of the Caisse de Dépôt. Perhaps that is why he had almost an almost fatherly attitude toward "his" Caisse. After participating in a few meetings of the board of directors meetings of the agency, André Marier sent the previously quoted 1978 letter to Marcel Cazavan which revealed a good deal about his intentions.

This letter, with all its lofty statements of principle was responsible in part for the creation some two years later of an activist investment policy at the Caisse. This policy would eventually result in losses of a magnitude never previously seen in the province of Quebec!

In 1966 and 1967, Claude Prieur again and again warned the young Caisse executives against the dangers of half-baked ideas coming from well-intentioned but inexperienced theoreticians. "Be wary, he was saying, of enthusiastic amateurs because their enthusiasm can be extremely costly."

Mr. Prieur proved to be right on the money. In 1980, with the arrival of a new board of directors, the nomination of Jean Campeau as President and the *en masse* resignations of the executives already in place, these "enthusiastic amateurs" would take control of the Caisse de Dépôt.

In retrospect, it is now also clear that the nomination of Jean Campeau as President and General Director in 1980 marked the beginning of the influence of the Parti Québécois government on the Caisse and of a policy of firm interventionism.

THE PÉQUISTE GOVERNMENT
TAKES CONTROL OF THE CAISSE DE DÉPÔT

This influence of the state on the Caisse de Dépôt had begun soon after the election of the Parti

Québécois in November 1976 and the nomination of Jacques Parizeau as Finance Minister of the province. The most imaginative of all the péquiste Ministers, M. Parizeau was well aware of the importance of the Caisse de Dépôt that was theoretically under the responsibility of his ministry. The Quebec government also had the power to nominate the members of the Caisse board of directors. From 1977 to 1979, the government named many new members favourable to the Parti Québécois on the board of directors. The most well-known of these members was Pierre Péladeau, the President of Québecor, and André Marier, an important civil servant and a special adviser to the Lévesque government. The new Caisse board of directors was very critical of General Manager Marcel Cazavan. After a while Mr. Cazavan agreed to resign before the end of his term in January 1980 and was replaced by Jean Campeau.

Mr. Campeau had previously worked as a Deputy Minister under the direction of Jacques Parizeau, then Finance Minister. He would go on working under the orders of the Finance Minister, but now as President and General Manager of the Caisse de Dépôt and as a Parti Québécois sympathizer.

Soon afterwards, Assistant General Manager Jean-Michel Paris was forced to resign by his immediate superior, Jean Campeau. The two men started to have problems getting along when, according to Mr. Paris, he discovered that after each meeting of the investment committee attended by the general managers and portfolio directors, Mr. Campeau would lock himself in his office for up to an hour, often during the lunch break, to make phone calls. According to Jean-Michel Paris, these calls were made to the Finance ministry in Quebec City and in particular to Jacques Parizeau who would give his personal directives, very often completely contradicting the decisions of the investment committee.

THE CAISSE EXECUTIVES ARE DISPATCHED

The long post-meeting phone conversations with Quebec City often had immediate and serious consequences. In the afternoon, Jean Campeau would, each time it became necessary, pay a visit to the individual committee members. He would then announce to them that important changes had to be made. Because of "new facts" that had come to his attention, certain of the morning's decisions would be "unmade" and the meeting minutes would have to be altered to reflect these changes. The situation soon became intolerable for Jean-Michel Paris. Disgusted with this transparent interference, he resigned during the summer of 1980.

Finally, between the end of 1980 and the beginning of 1981 there were other resignations among the Caisse's top brass. Jean Lavoie, the private placements director, decided to quit, as did his deputy. Raymond Lacourse, the Deputy Manager of the Caisse, also submitted his resignation with *his* deputy while Jean Laflamme, the fixed income portfolio director, and Gilles Doré, the real estate portfolio director also had to resign. The entire top echelon had been decapitated and was replaced by new executives with a bona fide "péquiste" allegiance.

THE RESIGNATION OF ERIC KIERANS

Trouble was brewing meanwhile at the board of directors of the Caisse. Eric Kierans, a former Finance Minister and Montreal Stock Exchange President, had been nominated to the board in October 1978. But he resigned with a resounding boom in 1980 when he learned about a particular decision of Jean Campeau. Mr. Campeau had negotiated with the Finance Minister Jacques Parizeau a loan to the Province of Quebec at a preferential rate. Mr. Kierans could not accept such a move which disadvantaged the Caisse for the profit of the Ministry of Finance. Jean Campeau had acted with the mentality of a former Deputy Finance Minister rather than as President of the supposedly independent Caisse de Dépôt. As a result of this controversial move, the Caisse lost in Eric Kierans an experienced director with the courage and means to denounce such abuses.

A NEW ROLE FOR JEAN CAMPEAU

In 1992 Mr. Campeau finally revealed his true political allegiance. He announced his decision to work for the Parti Québécois as President of Souveraineté Québec Inc., an organization connected with this party and collaborating with the "No" Committee for the October 1992 Referendum. Finally on

May 27, 1993 the leader of the Parti Québécois, Jacques Parizeau, proudly announced that the "great financier" Jean Campeau would be a PQ candidate in the next provincial election. It was, to make the analogy, just as if John Crow, President of the Bank of Canada, were to leave his position to run as a Tory candidate in the next federal election.

But the move was not completely disinterested. Jean Campeau will go on earning his annual fees of $150,000 from Domtar in accordance with the five-year contract he signed in 1991 when he became President of the board of directors of that corporation, even though he had to leave this position during the referendum campaign on the Canadian Constitution in 1992.

A NEW ORIENTATION FOR THE CAISSE

It is not, and I want to be very clear about this, not my intention to put the Caisse on trial in this book for its activities during the period when Jean Campeau was its President and General Director. I want, however, to bring out the facts, and they are both undeniable and pertinent: in the vast majority of cases, when the Caisse de Dépôt abandoned its proper independent, fiduciary role as manager of public funds to acquire politically-motivated significant positions in companies and consequently to intervene in the management of these companies, these investments turned into financial disasters for the Caisse and its depositors.

"Up to now, the successful transactions (like Provigo-Loeb and National Cablevision for example) seem to me so few that I have to ask myself if the Caisse does not have a strategy of dispersing its investments as much as possible so as to make its presence less noticeable. By acting this way, we will never be able to fundamentally modify the industrial structure of Quebec."[5]

André Marier's policy vision would soon be put into practice. Under the direction of Jean Campeau, the Caisse de Dépôt would turn itself into a conquering government agency, taking over responsibilities previously belonging to the S.D.I. (Quebec's Industrial Development Corporation) which did not have the capital to "fundamentally modify the industrial structure of Quebec" as André Marier's fateful sentence mandated in his by now well-known letter.

In order to support my analysis, allow me to present some concrete examples of investment decisions made by the Caisse de Dépôt. The first that comes to mind is the case of Provigo, one of the jewels of the Quebec food sector, a corporation now called Univa.

---

5   Letter addressed to Marcel Cazavan, President of the Caisse de Dépôt, by André Marier, March 17, 1978.

THE PROVIGO-UNIVA CASE

As a director of the variable income portfolio, I had bought for the Caisse de Dépôt more than 22% of the outstanding shares of Provigo. This company was the result of the merger of Denault of Sherbrooke, Couvrette & Pronovost of Montreal and Lamontagne of Chicoutimi. The President of Provigo was Antoine Turmel, a brilliant player in the food industry who had in fact orchestrated the merger. The cost of this investment was $6 million for the Caisse. When I left the Caisse in 1979, this investment had almost quadrupled and was worth nearly $24 million.

In concert with this acquisition, the stock portfolio purchased over the years a 26% interest in M. Loeb Ltd. Through subsidiary companies this Ontario food company enjoyed sales twice as big as those of Provigo, but it had lower profits. The total cost of this investment for the Caisse was $5.4 million. This amount was more than covered by the subsequent sale of M. Loeb to Provigo.

Following my nomination in 1976 as Senior Corporate Investment Advisor, a position involving company mergers and corporate governance, I was nominated to the board of directors of M. Loeb Ltd. When Bertram Loeb resigned as President of this corporation in 1978, I convinced the President of Provigo, Antoine Turmel, to buy the Caisse's interest in M. Loeb. This move allowed Mr. Turmel to become President of M. Loeb Ltd. and to start to integrate Provigo and Loeb, creating in the process a food chain giant. Some time later, the board of directors of Horne & Pitfield of Alberta (a subsidiary of M. Loeb that also controlled an important wholesaler in Northern California) accepted an offer of a share exchange with Provigo. As the Caisse already had an important interest in Horne & Pitfield, this meant it automatically increased its interest in Provigo.

This event also marked the beginning of the national and international vocation of Provigo. With M. Loeb Ltd., Provigo was now a significant presence in the markets of Ontario, Alberta and California.

Provigo seemed destined for a brilliant future. It was well managed by Pierre Lessard, who became its President in 1981. The company reached a record profitability, the value of its securities soared, and the result was an enormous capital gain for the Caisse de Dépôt.

Still, the nomination on the Provigo board of certain directors "suggested" by Jean Campeau progressively removed real control of the corporation from the hands of Antoine Turmel. But Turmel stubbornly refused to knuckle under to Campeau as the President of the Caisse de Dépôt had seemed to expect he would. The climax of this struggle between two men and their visions was reached when the board of directors of Provigo, in April 1985, chose Pierre Lortie as CEO and General Manager of Provigo. He was preferred over Pierre Lessard, a man with proven ability who had worked for the company for more than sixteen years.

This was an indeed an ironic choice: Pierre Lortie, while certainly an intelligent and dynamic man and a former president of the Montreal Stock Exchange, had no experience at all in the food sector. Pierre Lessard was equally intelligent and dynamic, and enjoyed in addition the benefit of his long experience with Provigo. To deal with this perceptual "difficulty" in distinguishing between the candidates' potential, a new slogan was launched by Jean Campeau's team: Pierre Lessard was now "the man of the past" and Pierre Lortie, the man of the present and of the future.

To help the reader to better understand the substance and meaning of these events, allow me to quote some excerpts from an article published in the December, 1989 issue of *Commerce* magazine:

> For Antoine Turmel, the Caisse de Dépôt and the Sobeys are the originators of the current problems of Provigo. On Friday afternoon, March 12, 1982, Jean Campeau declared to the President of Provigo that he had reached an agreement with the Sobeys. Under this agreement, the Caisse had increased its interest in Provigo to 30% and could make use of the voting rights attached to the 13% interest belonging to the Sobeys. In exchange for that, three seats on the board of directors were allocated to the Caisse and two to the Nova Scotia businessmen.

> Mr. Turmel: "I demanded some explanations from Jean Campeau. He answered that he did not want Provigo to be taken over by investors from out of Quebec. I was furious, and told him that

he had done just that when he had given the Sobeys an influence that I did not want to let them
have. To begin with, we would now be obliged to
hold our meetings in English because of their
presence. Moreover, we should not forget that
the Sobeys were our competitors in some areas. I
explicitly did not want them on the board of directors."

During the fall of 1984, Jean Campeau and Donald Sobey met twice with Pierre Lessard. Despite Lessard's undeniably good record, Campeau
and Sobey thought that they required a candidate with more strategic vision and panache to
succeed Antoine Turmel. "Unfortunately, Pierre
Lessard was never one for well-rounded rheto-
ric", Mr. Turmel willingly admitted.

In April 1985, the Caisse and the Sobeys made
their final choice. They hired Pierre Lortie to
succeed Antoine Turmel as CEO of Provigo.
"They were afraid of Pierre Lessard because he
was my pupil, said Antoine Turmel. During all
my years with Provigo, I always treated the
Caisse as an ordinary shareholder and this got
Jean Campeau's goat." When he learned of the
choice of Pierre Lortie, the retiring President of
Provigo gave a last piece of advice to Mr. Campeau: "I warned him, said Mr. Turmel. A winning
combination should not be broken up. Sooner or
later, you will have to pay for this mistake."

Jean Campeau was convinced that Provigo had come to a turning point in its history. The corporation, according to him, had to take a new orientation, embark on new paths. That is why the grandiose ideas of Pierre Lortie appealed so much to him.

Basically, Antoine Turmel declared that Pierre Lortie did not have the necessary experience to succeed him: "Under the market conditions, we knew that in California we could not be wholesalers as well as retailers. Pierre Lortie decided to do just the reverse and he is losing money at it. Sports Experts (a retailer of sports equipments) used to be a money-making proposition, but under Lortie's stewardship it is not any more."

The founding President of Provigo was also very critical of Pierre Lortie's investment decisions. "When I left Provigo in 1985 the company had cash in hand of over $100 million. This constituted a very enticing amount of money for a new and inexperienced chief executive officer. A month after taking office, Pierre Lortie dilapidated all the cash, by buying a controlling interest in Consumers' Distributing (CD)."

Antoine Turmel stated that he had also considered at some point buying CD, but rejected the idea: "This seemed clearly so bad a deal that I did not even present the proposal to the board. Pierre Lortie confirmed himself as an inexperienced manager by buying CD for an exorbitantly high price. He wanted to demonstrate to everybody that things were going to move at Provigo!" Mr. Turmel claimed that Mr. Lortie dug himself deeper into the hole by buying all the shares the corporation even after he realized the seriousness of the problems at CD.[6]

Antoine Turmel attributed most of the responsibility for the problems at Provigo to the Caisse: "When Provigo's board of directors was dominated by experienced managers with a good knowledge of the food retail business, everything was going well. The Caisse nominated its own people on the board, people who were not specialists in this sector."

In any event, Pierre Lessard was forced to resign in September 1985, shortly after the nomination of Pierre Lortie as President and General Director of Provigo. There could not be two bosses in the same company.

Mr. Lortie's tenure did not last long though. In 1988 Bertin Nadeau, the principal shareholder of Provigo, decided to accede to the presidency himself. According to one of the executives at Univa, the cost

---

6   Consumers' Distributing was sold in 1991 to European buyers; in 1992 Horne & Pitfield from Alberta was sold by Univa as well as the rights connected to the I.G.A. trademark in Ontario and Quebec's north-west to Oshawa Wholesale, an Ontario competitor.

of Lortie's management for Provigo was at least $300 million, not an inconsiderable amount.

All these changes had an effect on the corporation's profits. From a peak of $0.80 per share in 1988, the shareholders saw their earnings per share decrease to $0.71 in 1989, then plummet to $0.12 in 1990 and $0.01 in 1991. The earnings went up again to $0.57 in 1992 under the new management of Bertin Nadeau.

During that same period, Pierre Lessard, having been for two years President of Aeterna Life, was appointed to take charge of Métro-Richelieu. This food retail company was in serious difficulty because of an overwhelmingly high debt.[7] After years of hard work, Mr. Lessard was vindicated: the stock price of Métro-Richelieu soared at the Montreal Stock Exchange between January 1991 and December 1992 from $3.25 to $9.50 and the corporation's profits tripled during the same period. Meanwhile Provigo's stocks went down progressively, from $12.00 in 1988 to $7.50 at the end of 1992.

After these interventions in 1982 and 1984, Jean Campeau realized that corporate activism had a number of unexpected side benefits. People were

---

7   Before Pierre Lessard's nomination at Métro-Richelieu, the Caisse de Dépôt had thought of investing in the growth of this company in 1988 by buying bonds convertible in shares of Métro-Richelieu at $7.25. It would have amounted to the equivalent of more than 20% of the corporation's capitalization.

beginning to bow down in front of him. Mr. Campeau rapidly realized that with assets of $30 billion the Caisse de Dépôt was in a position to make waves in the financial milieu not only in Quebec, but also in the rest of Canada. The Caisse's President, who liked to call attention to his modest origins, had apparently discovered that power was in fact a stronger intoxicant than money — the principal motivation of his new capitalist friends.

From then on, the President of the Caisse gave a lot of leeway to his employees in the management of the general portfolio. With the help of his collaborators hired from the ministry of Finance, he was concentrating on the private placements portfolio. This way, the Caisse could intervene more directly in the management of companies.

The sorcerer's apprentices from the Caisse de Dépôt had unknowingly torpedoed Provigo, but they had changed their interlocutors from the team of Antoine Turmel-Pierre Lessard-Paul Gobeil[8] to the astonishing trio of Jean Campeau-Sobey-Unigesco.

---

8   Mr. Gobeil who was Vice-President, Finance of Provigo became Minister and president of the Treasury Board under the provincial Liberal government in 1985. In 1988 he co-authored a report that recommended measures to cut costs in government. His recommendations were never implemented by the government of Robert Bourassa.

THE SURPRISING CASE OF UNIGESCO

Unigesco is really the result of the ambition of one man, Bertin Nadeau, who took control of this small company in 1982. Mr. Nadeau comes from a New-Brunswick family and his father was involved in a small furniture factory. He graduated with a M.B.A. and a doctorate in management. Before becoming involved in Unigesco, Bertin Nadeau was a teacher at the École des Hautes Études Commerciales in Montreal. In 1985 the Régime d'Épargne Actions (R.E.A. or Quebec Stock Savings Plan/Q.S.S.P.) was in full swing and Bertin Nadeau realized its enormous potential. After a few small purchases of stocks in the food sector, he decided to plunge in head first.

At that time (1985) Jean Campeau had already concluded his alliance with the Sobeys. This alliance we recall, had brought in Pierre Lortie as president of Provigo and forced the resignation of Pierre Lessard. But Jean Campeau was somewhat ill at ease because he had put himself in the role of collaborating with the Sobey family of Nova Scotia and was already uncertain about the correctness of his choice of Pierre Lortie. The president of the Caisse de Dépôt was ready to distance himself from the controversy surrounding the management of Provigo.

So when Bertin Nadeau presented himself at the Caisse with his university degrees and his reputation as an intellectual and an entrepreneur, Jean Campeau decided to take him under his wing. Mr. Nadeau would be introduced into the inner circle of the Caisse de Dépôt as a manager, eventually allowing

41

the Caisse to get rid of the prickly dossier that Provigo had turned into.

The first manoeuvre of the Caisse de Dépôt involved the sale in 1985 of some 3,000,000 shares of Provigo to Unigesco for $45 million. Soon after, Unigesco bought an additional number of shares from the Banque Nationale and the Groupe Laurentien, acquiring a total interest of 4,500,00 shares.

In order to finance this deal which was worth $70 million, Mr. Nadeau used a group of stockbrokers to sell to the public 12,100,000 class B non-voting shares of Unigesco at the price of $5.00 per share. These shares had the not inconsequential advantage of being eligible for an income tax deduction of 150% under the Quebec Stock Savings Plan. This was because of the size of Unigesco, even if the product of the issue would be entirely applied to buy stock in Provigo, which was not eligible for these same deductions. Having succeeded in doing indirectly what he could not do directly, Bertin Nadeau was called a "financial genius" by Guy Desmarais, then president of Geoffrion Leclerc, one of his main investment bankers.

This reputation of financial genius would not last long though. From a profit peak of $13.5 million reached in 1987, the profits rapidly declined, mutating in fact into losses of $20 million in 1991 and $900,000 in 1992. The stocks followed that same downward trend, falling from $7.75 in 1987 to around $1.00 at the beginning of 1993.

Meanwhile Unigesco concluded its purchase of Provigo. Through a series of private transactions the corporation increased its interest in Provigo to 20% of the capitalization at an additional cost of $133 million. In 1989 an agreement was reached between Empire Company Ltd. (a company under the control of the Sobey family) and Unigesco. The two companies agreed to acquire together 8,500,000 shares of Provigo. This gave Unigesco an interest of 26% in Provigo and Empire, an interest of 25%. Bertin Nadeau had by this time become president of Provigo, following the departure of Pierre Lortie.

A great part of this transaction was financed by means of debt. At the end of 1992, despite a frenzied disposition of many of its assets, Unigesco still possessed as its main assets Red Carpet, a coffee distributor in western Canada, Sodisco, a hardware distributor (operating at low profit rates and purchased in 1990 for more than $150 million) and finally its interest of 26% in Provigo(Univa) — 22.5 million shares worth at that point only $7.50 per share or $170 million. With a consolidated debt of $340 million and some $60 million in payments due in June 1993, Unigesco was in dire straits.

The epithet of financial genius was once more mentioned in connection with Bertin Nadeau in February 1993. Mr. Nadeau had convinced a group of New York financiers, Blackstone Capital Partners to buy all the stock of Provigo (Univa). Blackstone would acquire the shares for $1.6 billion — $11.00

per share — using the assets of Provigo to obtain a loan for a good part of the buying cost.

Mr. Nadeau was trying to conclude a difficult transaction, which seemed all the more impressive when it became known that he was retaining the right to buy back a controlling interest in Univa from the Americans in three to seven years. This financial acrobatic manoeuvre was quite obviously motivated by the necessity to prevent an outcry from Quebec's nationalists, who would be certain to see this transaction as a sell-out of a national jewel to foreign interests. Unfortunately for Mr. Nadeau's plans, the new management now in place at the Caisse de Dépôt was not at all ready to be as agreeable in this case as were their predecessors during what became known as the "Steinberg affair," which was by now recognized everywhere in Quebec as a fiasco. Also, Bertin Nadeau had the improvidential idea of nominating Jean Campeau to the board of directors of Univa and Unigesco and this gesture of confidence would prove to backfire on him in a most unfortunate way.

Once more the Caisse de Dépôt used its power, now to make this new deal abort. They threatened Blackstone Capital Partners with court action even before an independent committee composed of directors of Univa could give its opinion on the merits of the deal. This kind of interventionism — coming from any quarter — is, in my opinion, always bad for business.

Let us recapitulate and examine now the consequences resulting from the initial decision of Jean Campeau to make an alliance with the Sobeys in 1982 and his other major act in 1985 in which Pierre Lessard was replaced as president of Provigo:

1. Unigesco now has a 100% interest in Sodisco and a group of small food distribution companies. After selling its stocks of Univa, its debt is around $170 million; this is probably less than the market value of its assets, but the corporation still has large debt repayments which it has difficulty meeting.

2. Univa (Provigo) was obliged to sell its strategic interests in Ontario and in Alberta which it had bought in 1977; this was necessary to lighten the debt load incurred by Provigo's presidents who had succeeded Antoine Turmel and Pierre Lessard.

3. Quebec was running the risk of giving control to foreign interests of a corporation which was formerly controlled by Quebecers. After announcing that the price of $11 per share offered by Blackstone to all shareholders was too low, the Caisse de Dépôt subsequently announced on June 13, 1993 that it was buying from Unigesco 26% of the shares of Univa for $8.50 per share! This would give the Caisse effective control of Univa with 37% of the shares, and the transaction allowed Unigesco to avoid going into default. Nevertheless the distasteful ruckus generated by the threats of the Caisse toward Black-

stone Capital Partners in this affair served to devaluate investments considered as "québécois" in the minds of foreign investors.

THE SOCANAV-STEINBERG SAGA

The purchase of the Steinberg stores by Socanav, a small shipping company, thanks to the Quebec Stock Savings Plan — with the help of the Caisse de Dépôt et Placement — developed into one of the most spectacular financial sagas in Quebec's history.

At the end of 1986, Michel Gaucher realized the potential of the Stock Savings Plan for small businessmen. Seeing the enormous popularity of this method of raising capital, he decided to list his small company, Socanav Inc. on the stock exchange and to issue 5,000,000 non-voting class A shares. The price was $5.00 per share and the sale would generate $25 million.

At the end of 1987, the sales of Socanav were around $43 million. The corporation used the new capital generated by its stock offering to buy a bus company and a steel distributor. This increased its sales to $141 million in 1988 and to $154 million in 1989. Unfortunately however, profits did not follow the same rate of increase. From a peak of $0.49 per share soon after the public stock offering, the profits fell to $0.41 in 1988 and $0.37 in 1989.

Michel Gaucher was consumed by a legitimate ambition. He did not see himself as operating a fleet of buses and small tankers for the rest of his life. He was also strongly influenced by the then-current trend of LBOs or leveraged buy-outs. Such purchases allowed certain american and canadian financiers — like Donald Trump and Robert Campeau for example — to buy important assets with the help of massive loans. In the spring of 1989, Pierre Laurin, General Director of Merrill Lynch Quebec, suggested to Mr. Gaucher that he consider buying the Steinberg stores. This Quebec jewel, went the pitch, could not "morally" be sold to Ontario investors as the Steinberg sisters, daughters of founder Sam Steinberg, were arguing. Michel Gaucher was very interested by this suggestion and started planning the purchase even if he had no previous experience in the food retailing business. Pierre Laurin, who had easy access to Jean Campeau, painted a rosy picture to him of all the benefits which would result from the Socanav-Caisse de Dépôt alliance in order to keep the control of Steinberg in the hands of Quebecers. But the first meeting between Jean Campeau and Michel Gaucher went nowhere. Mr. Campeau realized that an enormous contribution was expected of the Caisse for this deal to be concluded, and he decided to politely postpone his decision.

At that point, Pierre Laurin, who also knew that Jean Campeau wanted in a bad way to increase the real estate holdings of the Caisse de Dépôt, talked to him about the possibility of the deal going through in such a way that the Caisse would acquire the Ivanhoe real estate division of Steinberg on the condition that the Caisse would finance Socanav for its purchase of the whole Steinberg empire. Some of the advisers of the president at the Caisse de Dépôt were against this investment. When Mr. Laurin declared to Mr. Campeau though — and this was not a complete bluff, by the way — that Merrill Lynch Capital of New York was ready to finance such an investment, the CEO of the Caisse could not the resist the temptation of scoring a financial coup under the noses of the Americans by means of this daring investment. For Jean Campeau then, this purchase had a double advantage: first, it gave satisfaction to his masters in Quebec City and second, it shut out Oxdon Investments Inc. of Toronto. This corporation was still very much in the picture and had made an interesting offer to the Steinberg sisters, an offer which would not have required any financial contribution from the Caisse. Mr. Campeau wanted very much to get the Toronto businessmen out of the deal, and he was also worried that Merrill Lynch would do the financing alone. That is why he convinced his board of directors to go ahead and buy Steinberg jointly with Gaucher, who was the only Quebec entrepreneur willing to risk $25 million of his own money. The proposed strategy was that the Caisse would finance $820 million of the total cost of the transaction of $1.3 billion and buy $30 million worth of class A shares of Socanav. The total contribution of the Caisse for the transaction would come to $850 million. Included evidently in the $1.3 billion were $13 million in fees, of which a good part went to Merrill Lynch, Pierre Laurin's employer. The deal was finalized on August 21, 1989, a few months before the start of the current recession which has had a particularly devastating effect on businessmen who were too daring at the wrong time.

In 1989 the real estate markets were universally buoyant. The prices paid for real estate that year reached unequalled peaks. The Caisse de Dépôt was underweighted as compared to other financial institutions with respect to its real estate portfolio. So the purchase by the Caisse in March 1990 of the real estate division of Steinberg, called Ivanhoe Inc., at the cost of $887 million, contributed to a balancing of its portfolio holdings. With this purchase, the $850 million debt incurred by Socanav for the purchase of Steinberg's properties was erased. The Caisse also invested another $37 million in Steinberg while keeping its shares of Socanav bought for $30 million. Over the following years, another $100 million had to be invested in Ivanhoe Inc. in order to improve the real estate properties.

The Caisse de Dépôt had thus apparently connected with both punches:

1. The control of Steinberg was retained in Quebec, as Socanav had bested a offer made by Oxdon, the Toronto group connected with Gordon Capital.

2. An important real estate portfolio was obtained at a good price in the context of 1989. The properties in this portfolio were mainly shopping centres whose

principal lessees were the Steinberg grocery stores and the M department stores — both part of the Steinberg empire.

Unfortunately, this idyllic scenario would soon turn into a nightmare for the Caisse de Dépôt and for its protege, Michel Gaucher.

Without any experience in the distribution of food products and of general merchandise, Mr. Gaucher soon realized that the control premium paid for the Steinberg voting shares belonging to the Steinberg sisters had cost him too much, raising the price of the deal by $144 million. Mr. Gaucher had to begin a frenzied sale of assets in order to cover the interest on Steinberg's debt, the dividends on the preferred stocks and also to meet his obligation to buy back these preferred stocks. The best assets were easily sold, like the Miracle Food Mart division of Ontario for $227 million — a very high price. The jewel of the crown, a 50% share of Price Club (Canada), was sold off for $58 million — a reasonable price. Unfortunately for Mr. Gaucher, nobody wanted Smitty's, the Arizona subsidiary of Steinberg's that was losing money, nor the Valdi division that is still for sale.

In spite of the gigantic efforts deployed by Mr. Gaucher it was impossible to make Steinberg profitable. The corporation was crushed by its debt and did not succeed in selling off the money-losing general-merchandise M stores — formerly Miracle Mart. Meanwhile the Arizona market where Smitty's was operating was in the midst of a ferocious price war, transforming that division into a veritable millstone around Steinberg's neck.

Finally, at the beginning of 1992 the recession and the competition not having let up, Steinberg's situation became intolerable. Unable to go on, pressed by his creditors, Michel Gaucher had to abandon ship. Steinberg was placed under the protection of the Court while it tried to reach a settlement with its debt holders.

In May 1992, what was left of the Steinberg grocery store chain was divided between Métro-Richelieu (which bought about half of it) and Oshawa-Wholesale of Toronto and Provigo for the balance. The possible liquidation of the rest of the assets could eventually compensate at most 20% or 25% of the debt held by small non-guaranteed creditors who had been left high and dry by the bankruptcy. As for the big banks, they managed to minimize their losses in this misadventure.

The Société de Développement Industriel du Québec (where I worked as an administrator in 1978 and 1979) was asked to invest $50 million in Steinberg in 1989. Now, according to article 7 of its charter, all loans over $1 million must be approved by the Quebec Cabinet itself. This example shows just how high the decisions went, implicating the provincial Cabinet — Liberal at that time — in a decision to support a financial adventure with public funds.

The big loser in this affair though was the Caisse de Dépôt. Its $30 million investment in Socanav is now worth only a fraction of the price originally paid. The $70 million loan it made for the purchase of Steinberg Inc. will eventually result in a further loss of possibly $70 million. Finally, the purchase of Ivanhoe Inc., the real estate subsidiary of Steinberg, at a cost of $887 million gave the Caisse the ownership of shopping centres whose main lessees were usually Steinberg stores. This real estate subsidiary was badly hit by the recession that began at the end of 1989.

An agreement with the debt holders of Steinberg was tabled on November 24, 1992. Following this reorganization, many of the leases lapsed because of the closing of the Steinberg groceries stores and the bankruptcy of the M stores. According to an employee of the Caisse with whom I talked, Ivanhoe Inc. could be worth in 1993 only two-thirds of the price paid for it in 1989. Obviously, all the threads in this affair are a part of the same fabric. The Caisse de Dépôt could not anticipate in 1990 a "reorganization" of Steinberg that would lead to the cancellation of the leases held by Ivanhoe Inc., thus creating a devaluation of these real estate assets.

In 1991 the Caisse de Dépôt wrote off its investment in Steinberg for an amount of $130 million. A write-off of the real estate assets held by Ivanhoe Inc. was also taken at fair market value, partially explaining the 3.8 % negative return in the real estate portfolio of the Caisse de Dépôt for 1991.

Michel Gaucher's ambition was great, but by any standards, perfectly legitimate: he wanted to become

a captain of industry, controlling sales of many billion of dollars, with corresponding profits. Mr. Campeau, the trustee of Quebecers' savings, could have
and should have stopped Mr. Gaucher's ambition in
this case. His role should have been to favour a more
rational solution — even if it came from Ontario and
not from Quebec — because the investment
decisions of the Caisse de Dépôt should be regulated
by the interests of its depositors and not by an un-
avowed desire to "modify in the long term the industrial structures of Quebec".

TABLE I

ESTIMATED COST OF THE STEINBERG SAGA

1. FOR THE CAISSE DE DÉPÔT

(in millions of $)

December 1991	Steinberg write-off	130
December 1991	Socanav devaluation	26
December 1991	Devaluation of the Ivanhoe real estate portfolio	292
ESTIMATED TOTAL LOSS		448

2. FOR THE SOCIÉTÉ DE DÉVELOPPEMENT INDUSTRIEL DU QUÉBEC (S.D.I.)

(in millions of $)

December 1992	Estimated write-off	40

Source: Annual reports of Steinberg, Socanav and the Caisse de dépôt.

At the time of the "reorganization" of Steinberg Jean Campeau was already comfortably installed in his position as an administrator of Domtar, a company controlled by the S.G.F. (Société Générale de Financement) and the Caisse de Dépôt. Prior to that — from November 1990 to June 1991 — he had been respectively president of the board of directors of Domtar and co-president of the Bélanger-Campeau Commission. This commission had a mandate to consult Quebec's citizens about the Constitution and to make recommendations in this dossier to the government of Quebec.

THE BRASCADE EPIC

As soon as Jean Campeau took up his position at the Caisse de Dépôt in 1981, he developed the idea of increasing the influence of the agency that he was now directing by creating a veritable portfolio managed by the president called the participation portfolio.

During those years the Peter and Edward Bronfman brothers of Toronto were the darlings of the Canadian financial milieu. After gobbling up Canadian companies one after the other, the two businessmen were now targeting the prestigious Noranda Mines corporation as their next acquisition.

Noranda is a large mining company with its head office in Toronto. Though this company originated in Quebec, it had always been managed out of Toronto. Following its new strategy, the Caisse de Dépôt had become an important shareholder in Noranda. It had been rebuffed in trying to get one of its representatives elected to the board of directors of Noranda.

In the summer of 1981, it came to the knowledge of the Caisse de Dépôt that the Bronfman brothers of Toronto were trying to take control of Noranda. Jean Campeau then decided he wanted to be included in the exclusive club of the Bronfman's allies. Particularly in that he had been deeply insulted by the refusal of the president of Noranda, Alfred Powis, to give the Caisse a seat on his board of directors.

In order to win over these powerful potential allies, the Caisse offered to take an interest of 30% in the common shares of Brascade Resources Inc. This corporation was the financial holding that had the mandate to acquire control of Noranda Mines. The balance of the Brascade shares were held by Brascan, a company controlled by the Bronfman brothers.

The total cost of this transaction allowing the Caisse de Dépôt to penetrate into the prestigious fiefdom of the Bronfmans' was $450 million. Soon after the Caisse would exchange its stocks in Noranda and its stocks in Westmin for more stocks of Brascade. This deal gave it more than 15 million Brascade shares for a price of almost $40.00 per share or a total investment of more than $600 million.

In August 1981 Brascade succeeded in its takeover of Noranda. It did that with a purchase of 10 million common shares and 1.8 million preferred shares of the company. So the Caisse had acquired a minority interest of 30% in a holding (Brascade) that had taken control of 42% of Noranda. Mr. Campeau was also finally getting the much-coveted seat for the Caisse on the board of directors, but it came at a considerable cost. For the pleasure of outflanking Mr. Powis and obtaining a voice on Noranda's board of directors, the Caisse had become owner of $600 million worth of shares in a closed corporation that would never pay any dividends and would certainly create no capital gain.

The Caisse de Dépôt waited for more than seven years, without earning any dividends or capital gains for its investment in Brascade. The Caisse's executives finally realized that the real value of Brascade had been greatly exaggerated. Moreover, despite all their influence and the efforts to have more Francophones hired by Noranda Mines, the Executive Officers of that corporation were not convinced that this was the way to go. And yet, that consideration had been one of the main political motivations for the initial purchase of Brascade stocks by the Caisse de Dépôt.

In 1988, the Caisse de Dépôt had to concede that its position in Brascade was not very attractive. There was no advantage for the agency in being a minority shareholder in a holding whose common shares paid no dividends and that was not listed on the Stock Exchange. Also, the reputation of the Edper-Bronfman group of Toronto for being invincible was beginning to be seriously tarnished following the financial problems that it developed from 1987 on.

The Caisse de Dépôt had thus to extricate itself from that delicate situation. Therefore, on July 14 1988, the agency negotiated with the Bronfmans an exchange of half of its stocks in Brascade for 6.7 million shares of Noranda Mines. Finally on July 30, 1991 the Caisse ceded the rest of the Brascade stocks still in its possession for 4.1 million shares of Noranda. This manoeuvre brought the Caisse back to the starting point of August 1981, except that it now had taken a substantial loss as shown in Table II:

TABLE II
LOSS IN THE BRASCADE-NORANDA AFFAIR

(in millions of $)

Investment in Brascade from 1981 to 1983	600
LESS:	
Value of Noranda shares obtained in exchange for shares of Brascade in 1988 and in 1991	222
CAPITAL LOSS	378
PLUS:	
Lost revenue on the initial investment of $600 million, 8 years interest at the current rate of return of 10 %	480
TOTAL LOSS	**858**

Sources: Annual Reports of Brascade, Caisse de dépôt press releases.

THE DOMTAR CONQUEST

When I left the Caisse de Dépôt in 1979, the agency had in its portfolio 1,600,000 shares of Domtar bought at an average price of around $4.00 per share. This represented an amount of $6.5 million, a normal investment considering the magnitude of the Caisse's portfolio. But even then the interventionist pressures had begun to be exerted on then president Marcel Cazavan. Mr. Cazavan was more and more worried about the reactions of the Minister of Finance Jacques Parizeau and of his own board of directors flowing from his passive approach to the market. He then apparently decided to score a spectacular "coup" in June 1979. Not long after I resigned from my position at the Caisse, the agency bought in one shot a block of 2.8 million shares of Domtar from MacMillan-Bloedel at the high price of $27.00 per share. The total cost of the transaction was $75.6 million.

The Caisse de Dépôt now owned almost 22% of the Domtar stock. This constituted the first chapter of a long series of manœuvers that would end with full control of Domtar. The Caisse would wait however, until the arrival of Jean Campeau as its president in January 1980, to begin the process of transforming itself into a financial conglomerate ready to "surpass Paul Desmarais", a man much admired by Mr. Campeau.

Almost immediately, the new president of the Caisse proceeded to buy 600,000 shares of Domtar at an approximate cost of $15 million. This purchase upped the ante for the agency, whose investment in Domtar alone was now a massive $97 million-plus.

Under the guidance of Jean Campeau, in 1980, the Caisse de Dépôt transferred its interest in Domtar to the newly created participation portfolio that was, in fact, the president's toy. Mr. Campeau's new portfolio enabled him to increase the interest of the Caisse de Dépôt in Domtar from 22% to 26% and at the same time start to undermine the positions of the executive officers of this corporation.

Jean Campeau did not have long to wait for a counter-move. During a visit at the Caisse soon after this new purchase, Domtar's President and General Manager Alex Hamilton announced that he had important news to tell the big shareholder. He stated that it had become necessary for Domtar to issue more stock in order to bear the cost of a rapid expansion — particularly at its new fine paper mill in Windsor Mills, Quebec.

The Caisse had just invested more than $97 million, but not one penny of that amount had filtered into the depleted Domtar treasury. That money had been paid in large part instead to MacMillan-Bloedel and to its shareholders.

Jean Campeau wanted to act rapidly, because he believed that the interest of the Caisse de Dépôt in Domtar would be reduced to 13% due to the important dilution proposed by the executive officers of the corporation. The Caisse would have been more than welcome to invest in a new share issue — who would refuse $100 million? This would have provided the necessary capital and kept at 22% the percentage of the stock previously owned by the agency. Instead, Mr. Campeau had a series of consult-ations with the ministry of Finance. These led him to finally locate a partner who would be able to buy enough shares of Domtar to participate in a joint takeover, without the Caisse de Dépôt being obliged to go over its allowed investment cap of 30%. The unlucky partner designated by the province's politi-cal masters was the Société Générale de Financement (S.G.F.), the oldest of the state agencies involved in the industrial development of Quebec.

Domtar had fallen into disfavour with Finance Minister Jacques Parizeau because of the incon-siderate transfer of a minor head office to Toronto. Following the opening of a salt mine in the Magdelen Islands by Mine Seleine — a state agency —, the Domtar Sifto Salt subsidiary — 100% owned — had decided to move its operations from Montreal to Toronto. This would entail the transfer of a grand total of seventeen jobs. On December 2, 1980 in the National Assembly, Mr. Parizeau declared in a swift and bitter reaction: "We will have to find rules under which Quebecers' money will serve the best interest of Quebecers."

The provincial Minister of Finance decided in fact to punish Domtar for its role in the transfer of Sifto's head office to Toronto. By using the resources of the state agencies under his authority, he now intended to take control of Domtar. In retrospect, is seems ironic that, in order to avenge the loss of seventeen jobs, one of the most costly transactions in the history of the Caisse de Dépôt and of the S.G.F. was about to take place.

With the approval of Mr. Parizeau, the Caisse's President requested the assistance of Paul Desmarais, the head of Power Corporation. Mr. Desmarais decided to deal with Mr. Campeau, who was representing the S.G.F., by selling him all the shares of Domtar held by Power Corporation and its subsidiary corporations. Moreover, with secret offers to four other financial institutions, the Caisse obtained on August 18, 1981 an additional interest of 20% in Domtar, at the average price of around $32.00 per share. Less than nine months later the shares were trading below $20.00. This represented a loss of more than $100 million on the S.G.F. investment and of more than $120 million on the Caisse's investment. Obliged to cover the financial losses of Domtar, S.G.F. and Caisse de Dépôt had to invest additional amounts of $131 million to help Domtar go through what was a very difficult period.

Around the same time — during the spring of 1982 — I attended a luncheon of an association connected with the École des Hautes Études Commerciales (H.E.C.) in Montreal. The guest speaker was Jean Campeau, who I was meeting for the first time. During his speech, a proud Mr. Campeau announced that the stock portfolio of the Caisse de Dépôt now possessed two investments — Domtar and Brascade — that he himself described as "jewels of the crown" to the otherwise well-informed audience of the Association of the H.E.C.

According to my estimates, the Domtar "jewel" would eventually cost the depositors of the Caisse the "princely" sum of $117.2 million by the end of 1992. This is how I arrive at that figure: starting with a position in the portfolio in April 1989 of 1,600,00 shares at the initial cost of $4.25 per share, the Caisse would acquire afterwards — from 1979 to 1992 — enough shares to own about 20% of the stock issued by Domtar, or 24,823,000 shares with a market value on December 31, 1992 of $130.3 million — an estimated drop in value of $117.2 million.

Also, this investment — even when devalued year after year — has the disadvantage of earning no dividends (since 1991). And Domtar will have to wait for a visible improvement of its financial health before paying any dividends at all. As the Caisse could earn around 8% on its regular investments, there is an income loss for the Caisse de Dépôt of $10.4 million per year on the market value of the investment as of December 31, 1992. This lost revenue would come to almost $18 million annually calculated on the estimated cost of the investment in Domtar at the same date.

POWER CORPORATION AND DOMTAR

In 1988, at the time when the Caisse de Dépôt owned about 20% of Domtar stock, Paul Desmarais of Power Corporation controlled 42% of the stock of Consolidated-Bathurst (C.B.). Mr. Desmarais came to the conclusion that it would be desirable for him to consider the merger of Consolidated-Bathurst with Domtar.

The executive officers of C.B. were convinced that they could substantially lower operating costs of the enterprise resulting from the merger of C.B. with Domtar. Particularly in that the products made by the two companies seemed to complement each other — fine papers and building supplies for Domtar, newsprint paper and cardboard for Consolidated-Bathurst.

It was obvious though, that thorough preparations had to be made in order to spare the feelings of Quebec's nationalists, who would be sure to see the takeover by Power Corporation of a company controlled by the Société Générale de Financement and the Caisse de Dépôt, as a significant negative.

For that reason, there were major changes in the executive offices of Consolidated-Bathurst. Then the board of directors, on which I sat, was called to approve the nomination of Guy Coulombe as new President of the corporation during the fall of 1988. Mr. Coulombe had pursued a career that placed him squarely in among the prominent members of Quebec Inc. After a career as a senior bureaucrat in Quebec City, he became President of S.G.F. and then of Hydro-Québec. Finally he was hired as President of Consolidated-Bathurst in the fall of 1988.

It was a signal day for Consolidated-Bathurst: for the first time in its history, the corporation was headed by a Francophone Quebecer. Despite the fact that this kind of parachute-drop nomination was fraught with danger for the morale of his employees, Paul Desmarais was well aware of what he was doing. To be able to absorb Domtar, he had to francicize C.-B., whose management at that time was not particularly overflowing with Francophone executives. The game plan called for a strategy in which the executive officers of Consolidated-Bathurst would manage both of the merged corporations.

And so Power Corporation began a series of negotiations with the Caisse de Dépôt, which had abrogated to itself the right to speak in the name of the S.G.F. Jean Campeau, for his part, did not share Power Corporation's vision of the Connie Bathurst management supplanting the Domtar executive suite. He had previously talked of his interest in Domtar as a "jewel". He did not want to relinquish control of Domtar to Power corporation via an exchange of shares between the two corporation that had every probability of putting Domtar at a disadvantage.

Fortune was about to smile once more on Paul Desmarais, who was suddenly, in January 1989, in possession of a major negotiating chip which served to accelerate the merger talks. He had just received a firm offer from Stone Container of Chicago, good for only 48 hours, for 100% of the stock of Consolidated-Bathurst. Stone was offering $25 per share — a total amount of $2.6 billion. Despite this attractive offer, Mr. Desmarais was still interested in the C.-B./Domtar merger, but because of the extremely tight deadline imposed by Stone, he had to negotiate rapidly.

Mr. Desmarais, concerned by the attitude of the Caisse which had refused the share swap based on the respective market values of the Domtar and C.-B. stock, went straight to the top. The President of Power Corporation decided to put his case directly to Quebec premier Robert Bourassa, but the indecisive premier did not want to implicate himself directly in this affair, and he referred Mr. Desmarais back to Jean Campeau.

The negotiations were restarted in a hurry. And even though they continued late into the night, the Caisse de Dépôt and the team of Power Corporation/Consolidated-Bathurst did not reach an agreement. Despite the Stone Container offer of $25 per share that improved the value of the stock of C.-B., the stumbling block remained the rates of the respective share exchange based on the stock exchange prices. The President of the Caisse — to whom the provincial cabinet had tossed this "hot potato" — finally rejected the terms of the exchange proposed by Power Corporation, and killed the deal.

In the end, the rejection of the deal by Mr. Campeau was a boon to Power Corporation. It accepted the Stone Container offer and the sale of C.-B. produced a cash windfall of $1.1 billion. It also allowed the corporation to avoid the difficult times that would soon befall both paper companies. As for Stone Containers, the unlucky buyer of Consolidated-Bathurst, it saw its stock fall from $32 in 1989 to $8 in 1993, and its debt instruments were also put on a watch list by Wall Street.

After the Caisse de Dépôt rejected the deal with Power Corporation, Jean Campeau had about one year left before the end of his term as its President. He had already set his mind on the presidency of the board of directors of Domtar as his next job. But he knew that, if the C.-B./Domtar merger became reality, Power Corporation would demand the management of the merged society for Consolidated-Bathurst. In that context, Mr. Campeau would never have become President of the board of the corporation resulting from the C.-B./Domtar merger. In the end, Mr. Campeau got the plum he wanted. When he left the Caisse de Dépôt at the beginning of 1990, he became President of the board of Domtar with all the privileges inherent to this position.

Unbeknownst to Jean Campeau, the former President of the Caisse had saved Paul Desmarais from an awful predicament. Without the sale to Stone Containers, Power Corp. would have had to shoulder the full responsibility of covering the massive losses taken by Domtar and Consolidated-Bathurst since 1989. Besides which, the new owners would have had to comply with ever-costlier new environmental standards. For Domtar alone, these would entail capital expenditures of more than $240 million over the next five years.

Everything went very well for Power Corporation, in the end. The losses of Consolidated-Bathurst are in the lap of the American shareholders, and those of Domtar — just as important — have to be paid by the shareholders of Domtar; among these are S.G.F.

(Quebec's taxpayers) and the Caisse de Dépôt (Quebec's pensioners). So the big winner in this affair, Power Corporation, consoled itself for its "defeat" by cashing a cheque of $1.1 billion at the beginning of June 1989. The Caisse, along with numerous small shareholders, received $25 per share for its stock in C.-B. (a total of $70 million for the agency).

GAZ MÉTROPOLITAIN

In 1976, because of my new responsibilities at the Caisse de Dépôt I was called on to serve on the board of directors of Gaz Métropolitain, where I remained until the beginning of 1980.

Toronto-based Norcen owned 85% of this natural gas distribution company, which had successfully fulfilled its role as the natural gas distributor in the Montreal area. Sensitive to its linguistic environment, Gaz Métropolitain and its executive offices had been voluntarily francicized before any langauge laws had come into effect. From time to time, the company would require the financial help of Norcen, as it was undercapitalized with respect to its various major investment projects.

This utility was governed by the *Régie du Gaz et de l'Électricité*, the board which had the power to decide on new tariff increases and on the allowed return on the utility's capital. The corporation earned stable profits, and its shares on the stock exchange were also stable (they had not fluctuated significantly over the course of ten years). This was normal for a public utility.

In 1980 Norcen changed hands and became the property of Conrad Black, the Toronto financier and owner of Argus Corporation. But Mr. Black's ambitions went far beyond the limitations placed on management of a public utility company distributing natural gas in Quebec. So when Jean Campeau, then President of the Caisse de Dépôt, heard that Gaz Métropolitain was a rising star and called Conrad Black to express his interest in acquiring some stock, the latter was all ears. At the end of 1980, Mr. Black sold to the Caisse de Dépôt the 65% controlling share of Gaz Métropolitain held by Norcen, at a price of $119 million. So a relatively important amount was paid to Norcen by the Caisse, but as in the case of Domtar, once again no money from the sale was used for the expansion of the newly-bought company.

As the Caisse de Dépôt was not allowed to own more than 30% of the stock of a corporation, it had to find itself a partner for Gaz Métropolitain, a partner who would, as in the Domtar takeover, purchase the balance of the stock required. Mr. Campeau used his contacts in the provincial government to obtain the assurances of the Minister of Energy and Resources, Yves Bérubé, that the state-owned agency SOQUIP (Société Québécoise d'Initiatives Pétrolières) would be ready to buy 35% of the stock at a cost of $64 million.

But there was one small hitch: SOQUIP did not have the necessary capital with which to buy the stock. A complex method involving the creation of a holding had to be invented to allow the deal to proceed until a permanent solution could be found. Using as an intermediary the brokerage firm of Lévesque Beaubien, the stock over and above the allowed 30% cap was bought, with a first right of repurchase by the Caisse de Dépôt. In essence, the shares were "parked" until a way could be found to deal with the problem. This transaction gave the Caisse control of a public utility company already under the regulatory control of the Régie du Gaz et de l'Électricité at a relatively advantageous price. The shares were bought initially using bonds earning interest at 12%. Eventually, with the cooperation of SOQUIP, the Caisse de Dépôt bought stock in Noverco — the holding controlling Gaz Métropolitain. The two state agencies then changed Gaz Métropolitain's legal status, making it into a limited partnership and issued a call for offers from prospective industrial partners.

Despite the difficulty in analyzing the results of this investment's permutations — from Gaz Métropolitain's initial status to a limited partnership — it seems that it has been profitable for the Caisse de Dépôt et Placement.

THE PARTICIPATION PORTFOLIO

Soon after my arrival at the Caisse de Dépôt, Claude Prieur — then its President — decided to create a new portfolio called Private Placements. this portfolio was mandated to finance companies that were not public — but could become so — by a combination of purchases of shares and also of bonds secured by the corporation's assets.

When the corporation was then registered on the stock exchange, the investment was then to be transferred to the general stock portfolio. Exceptionally, the private investment portfolio could buy an interest in corporations involving the sale by existing shareholders. The best-known investment of this kind was made in 1971 under the guidance of Gérard Cloutier — then Co-Managing Director of the Caisse de Dépôt — in a corporation called National Cablevision. This cable distribution company was at that time owned by American interests. Because of a new rule of the CRTC (Canadian Radio and Television Council) that did not allow foreigners to own more than 25% of a television or cable distribution company, these American investors had to divest their interest to Canadians. At the same time, a consortium, composed of various Quebec financial institutions, was created on the initiative of the Caisse de Dépôt in order to buy National Cablevision. The Caisse was here operating under the constraint of maximum holdings in any one company of 30%, so that the balance (70%) had to be shared among other Quebec savings institutions.

Later, in 1980, but before the departure of the executive officers in place at the Caisse, these National Cablevision shares were exchanged for Vidéotron stock. Vidéotron went public shortly thereafter, creating a huge capital gain on the initial investment of the Caisse de Dépôt, made in 1971, and which totalled less than $4 million. This windfall gave rise to considerable bragging by Jean Campeau and the new management of the Caisse, who conveniently forgot that it was because of the "old gang" — as Jean Campeau called them — that this initial investment had been made.

When Mr. Campeau arrived at the Caisse, the name of the private placements portfolio was changed to the "participation" portfolio. All the investments of the Caisse de Dépôt listed on the stock exchange that were of a special interest to the President were placed in that portfolio. These included Provigo (Univa), Domtar and C.P. (Canadian Pacific). This allowed Mr. Campeau and his newly-hired aides to put under their personal control the management decisions concerning these investments, rather than leaving them to the portfolio managers who had no political agenda and whose only priorities would have been to maximize the gains.

For the executives already in place at the Caisse, the newfound political activism of the institution made life more and more uncomfortable. They had serious, inflammatory arguments with Campeau over their predicted disastrous consequences that would result if the Caisse stuck to the new, activist strategy. For example, they were convinced of the folly of persisting in investing massively in Brascade and Domtar against the advice of the Caisse's own analysts. Their warnings were ignored, they fell afoul of the President, and they had to resign before the end of 1980.

Jean Campeau, now that he was the uncontested captain of the ship, saw himself as one of Canada's financial magnates. He quickly forgot that the objectives of a pension fund like the Régie des Rentes du Québec were very different than those of a private entrepreneur. These latter have their own control and acquisitions scenarios, which in fact are very often the opposite of the objectives and strategies of a pension fund.

In a speech in Toronto on February 28, 1983 Mr. Campeau observed: "If an investment is profitable for my partners at Brascan or for my friend Paul Desmarais, it will also be profitable for the Caisse de Dépôt."

With the help of the Caisse de Dépôt, Brascan did indeed succeed in taking control of Noranda Mines. Paul Desmarais was more than happy to get rid of his stock in Domtar when the Caisse de Dépôt and the unlucky S.G.F. decided to pay a high price to get the partial control of that company. In both cases, the objectives of the Caisse de Dépôt could not really coincide with those of Brascan, the majority shareholder of Brascade, nor with those of Power Corporation, the prime shareholder of Domtar. This was amply demonstrated by subsequent events.

If all the money sunk into Domtar or Brascade (Noranda) had at least served to set these businesses afloat again (thanks to all the Caisse's millions), this would have resulted in two companies with good capitalization and minimum debts. Instead of that, the major part of the Domtar investment went into the coffers of MacMillan-Bloedel at the end of 1979. And in 1980, into the subsidiary companies of Power Corporation when they sold their interest in Domtar directly to the Caisse de Dépôt. Of the $248 million invested by the Caisse, only $79 million — less than one third — reached Domtar's treasury. We could also conclude that in the case of Brascade, $450 million of the investment represented a net contribution of capital. However, the enormous amount paid was used for buying existing shares of Noranda; as far as Noranda's treasury was concerned, this transaction was of little practical benefit.

This adventure leads me to conclude that the kind of investments made in the participation portfolio of the Caisse should only be made — except for exceptional circumstances — in new shares of corporations and that these investments should be transferred in the general stock portfolio when these same shares are registered on the stock exchange.

THE COST OF INTERVENTIONISM
FOR THE CAISSE DE DÉPÔT

1. PROVIGO-UNIVA

The position of more than 22% of Provigo's capital bought by the team of Claude Prieur well before the nomination of Jean Campeau to the Caisse was bought for such a low price that it constituted for the Caisse an important source of capital gain even if the numerous permutations between Sobey and Unigesco subsequently diminished its value. It is impossible to estimate the diminished value of the Caisse's investment, except that clearly, without the intervention of the Caisse, Provigo would have been a lot more profitable and its shares on the stock exchange would certainly have traded at a higher price. Without Jean Campeau's interventionist policy, the Caisse would not have had to agonize in the winter of 1993 over consequences of the possible sale of Univa to Americans in order to set Provigo's majority shareholder — Unigesco — afloat again.

2. STEINBERG-SOCANAV

It is easier to estimate the loss in this investment: $448 million for the Caisse de Dépôt and $44 million for the S.D.I. (see Table I).

3. BRASCADE

The estimated loss for the Caisse de Dépôt — including lost interest for eight years — is $858 million (see Table II).

4. DOMTAR

We can estimate at $10.52 per share the cost of Domtar for the Société Générale de Financement. This total is obtained by going through the financial statements of S.G.F., but the same total could be arrived at in going through the financial statements of the Caisse de Dépôt.

Based on the fact that when I left the Caisse in 1979 there was an investment of $6.8 million in Domtar — about 1,600,000 shares at a cost of $4.25 each — I estimate that the Caisse has paid around $10.00 per share for its 24,823,000 shares of Domtar as of December 31, 1992.

TABLE III
LOSS IN THE DOMTAR ADVENTURE

	(in millions of $)
Domtar acquisition cost	248,0
Less: current market value of shares	130,8
LOSS	117,2

Note: These figures do not include compensation for lost interest, because Domtar declared dividend payments until 1991.

TABLE IV
TOTAL LOSSES ATTRIBUTABLE
TO INTERVENTIONISM
(recap estimates as of 31 december 1992)

1. Loss for the Caisse de Dépôt

	(in millions of $)
Steinberg-Socanav	448,0
Brascade	858,0
Domtar	117,2
TOTAL	1 423,2

2. Loss for the S.D.I.

Steinberg-Socanav	40
Domtar	50
TOTAL	90

3: Loss for the S.G.F. group

Domtar	150

By adding up the three above, we arrive at a total loss estimated for the government agencies involved in the financial transactions related to Steinberg-Socanav, Brascade and Domtar of $1663 million ($1.63 billion).

THE CAISSE DE DÉPÔT AND ITS INDEPENDENCE
FROM POLITICAL POWER

In 1991 the provincial Liberal government had Jean-Claude Delorme — a respected administrator from the business sector but with no experience in investment management — nominated as Chairman of the Caisse de Dépôt. Some time later the political powers that be had Guy Savard nominated to the newly-created position of President and Chief Operating Officer. This chartered accountant and business executive from Sherbrooke was a former organizer for the Liberal Party and he was well known as a real estate entrepreneur in the Magog area.

It is discouraging to see that these nominations, despite the individual value of the candidates, perpetuated the influence of provincial political power on the Caisse de Dépôt, with all the negative consequences brought about by such a situation. There have been rumours to the effect that the Caisse's operations were sometimes paralysed by disagreements between the executives hired by Jean Campeau and those more recently nominated by the provincial Liberal government.

This governmental interference at the Caisse de Dépôt starting with the Parti Québécois — who initiated that trend — as well as from the Liberal Party — who now had nominated a former Liberal organizer to an important position — could have the needless and unwarranted consequences of bringing on administrative paralysis in this key financial player in Quebec's economy.

We can even imagine a comic situation, supposing an electoral victory the Parti Québécois in the coming 1994 vote, with more political nominations at the Caisse made to counter the one of Mr. Savard. There has to be an end to this parade. We have to stop this process that has a tendency to distort the legislators' intention of 1965 concerning the Caisse's necessary independence from political influence — influence that can be particularly harmful, as I have shown.

THE MONOPOLY OF SAVINGS MANAGEMENT

As the years went by, the Caisse de Dépôt has become in fact the institution managing the entirety of the pension plans and public funds in Quebec. This monopoly management by the Caisse — no freedom of choice is given to the depositing funds — was approved under the laws voted by the Quebec's National Assembly.

The following table, taken from the annual report (December 31, 1992) of the Caisse de Dépôt, shows the depositors' investments in the Caisse — the main one being the Régie des Rentes du Québec. Listed below this first depositor are eleven other institutions that have been successively obliged to use the Caisse de Dépôt as years went by.

TABLE V: DEPOSITOR EQUITY
IN THE CAISSE DE DÉPÔT AS OF 12/31/92

Depositor (Translated where English names exist)	Abbr.	Initial deposit	Number of contributors[1]	Contributors' equity[2]
Régie des rentes du Québec	R.R.Q.	1966	2 999 200	15 200.7
COMMISSION ADMINISTRATIVE DES RÉGIMES DE RETRAITE ET D'ASSURANCE: Government and Public Employees Retirement Plan	CARRA RREGOP	1973	490 000	12 895.0
General Retirement Plan for Mayors or Councillors of Municipalities		1975	—	—
Individual Plans		1977	500	42.2
Pension Plan for Elected Municipal Officers		1989	2 200	79.1
Quebec Automobile Insurance Agency	SAAQ	1978	4 165 000	5 328.0
Commission de la santé et de la sécurité du travail	C.S.S.T	1973	184 030	3 834.6
COMMISSION DE LA CONSTRUCTION AU QUÉBEC Supplemental Pension Plan for Employees of the Quebec Construction Industry	C.C.Q.	1970	95 000	3 753.1
Fonds d'assurance-prêts agricoles et forestiers	FAPAF	1978	1	23.5
Régie des assurances agricoles du Québec		1968	49 488	—
Régie des marchés agricoles et alimentaires du Québec	RMAAQ	1967	58	3.0
Régime de l'assurance-dépôt du Québec		1969	1 384	120.6
La Fédération des producteurs de bovins du Québec		1989	26 286	1.0
Régime complémentaire de rentes des techniciens ambulanciers oeuvrant au Québec	RRRTAQ	1990	3 093	19.3
Office de la protection du consommateur Fonds des cautionnements collectifs des agents de voyages	OPC	1992	1 000	7.1

(1) estimate (2) market value in millions of dollars

In the beginning, the aim of the Caisse de Dépôt was to manage the Régie des Rentes du Québec. Later on, the legislators decided to use it to centralize the management of the numerous public and para-public funds of Quebec. The depositors listed in Table V had no freedom to choose where to invest their money and are, according to the statute, virtual prisoners of the Caisse de Dépôt.

The sheer size of the Caisse de Dépôt becomes also a hurdle for maximizing the returns on the money deposited by these different institutions — *i.e. the reason for the existence of any fund management.* When we consider the comparative returns on the investments of the Caisse we realize that, except for the real estate portfolio that has a very small annual compound interest of 1.5% for five years, the different portfolios have performed marginally better than the reference indexes. For a period of five years the returns on the bond investments are 12.7% for the Caisse de Dépôt and 12.3% for the Scotia McLeod index, on Canadian stocks 5.9% for the Caisse and 4.9% for the TSE 300 index, on foreign stocks 6% for the Caisse and 4.9% for the Morgan Stanley index, and finally on mortgage financing 12.5% for the Caisse and 12.2% for the Scotia McLeod index.

These comparative results though, do not have much practical value. People do not entrust a fund manager with their money to earn the rate of the Toronto Stock Exchange index. What they really want is to gain an added value resulting from an investment strategy that does not have much in common with the indexes.

That is why the most useful comparison would the one between the performance of the Caisse de Dépôt and different managed funds. In this way we could really establish if the Caisse has done better or worse than the other managers. According to this somewhat more appropriate method, it becomes evident that the Caisse de Dépôt has a performance well under the average of the Canadian managers as to return obtained with a diversified portfolio during the last five years and for the year 1992. To demonstrate this I will use the fund evaluation figures of S.E.I. in order to estimate the comparative return rate of the Caisse de Dépôt.

TABLE VI
COMPARATIVE RETURNS ON MANAGED FUNDS

	Year 1992	Annual composite rate for 5 years 1988-1992
Caisse de dépôt, total investments	4,5 %	9,7 %
S.E.I., composite of diversified funds		
First quartile	7,8 %	10,0%
Median	5,9 %	9,9 %
Third quartile	4,9 %	9,4 %

Sources: Annual reports of the Caisse de dépôt and S.E.I.

83

We are able to see that the returns obtained by the first quartile — the 25 best out of a hundred — of the whole of the diversified funds reporting to the S.E.I. are much higher than the returns obtained by the Caisse de Dépôt for the year 1992 and the period 1988-1992.

As for the rates obtained by the median of the funds, it is still higher than the rate of the Caisse for 1992 and slightly higher for the five-year period. The Caisse de Dépôt would in fact be placed among the managers at the "bottom of the class," i.e. in the third quartile[9]. The Caisse de Dépôt in a spirit of openness should put the emphasis in its annual report on measures of absolute and comparative return instead of giving an abundance of data on the breakdown of the portfolio.

Many would say that the huge size of the Caisse is a barrier to a better performance. This becomes evident when we compare the size of the Caisse relative to the Canadian economy and the American economy. With assets at market value of more than $41 billion, the Caisse de Dépôt exerts too much weight on Quebec's economy. By comparison, the biggest funds manager in the United States is a semi-public agency named CALPER that invests the pension funds of the employees of the state of California.

---

9   Without the losses of $1.4 billion generated by the Caisse's interventionism, the agency would have obtained an annual return of almost 1% higher for the years 1988-1992 which would place it in the first quartile of the diversified funds.

This agency manages four times the Caisse's assets, about $160 billion, but it is operating in the context of an economy forty times bigger than Quebec's and eleven times bigger than the whole Canadian economy.

If we use a comparison between Canada and the United States, the Caisse de Dépôt would theoretically have assets of $451 billion, almost three times as much as CALPER with its $160 billion under management. The size of the Caisse is in reality much too big for the financial markets of Quebec and that is why it is omnipresent in the economic life of the province. An entrepreneur who is not accepted by the Caisse de Dépôt has no other institutions of a comparable size where he could go to get financial backing. And when the Caisse de Dépôt decides to boycott a certain entrepreneur, he is completely in the Caisse's power and this could put him in a very difficult situation (see the text on Unigesco). The huge size of the Caisse de Dépôt necessarily translates into a lot of problems in the maximization of returns for the depositors who are, we recall, obliged by law to stay with the Caisse.

There are in Quebec many funds management firms administered by francophone and anglophone Quebecers. These firms would be undeniably qualified to bid for the management of the depositors' funds — other than the Régie des Rentes du Québec — that are presently managed by the Caisse de Dépôt. The mandates obtained through such public bidding would be based on five-year management contracts renewable in five-year terms as decided by depositors. I am convinced that a rational approach allows us to conclude that depositors — except for the R.R.Q. — should have the possibility of entrusting their savings and pension plans to managers of their choice, including managers at the Caisse de Dépôt. The yields obtained by other pension fund managers have often been higher than those obtained by the Caisse de Dépôt, whose gigantic size hinders its performance in ways already mentioned.

In one aspect, the huge size of the Caisse should theoretically give it an edge with respect to the ratio of its administration fees compared to the funds managed. Unfortunately it is not the case: after many years of stability the Caisse's administrative fees have increased from .058% in 1989 to .094% in 1992 as shown in Table VII.

TABLE VII
EVOLUTION OF MANAGEMENT FEES
OVER THE LAST FIVE YEARS

				(in millions of $)	
	1992	1991	1990	1989	1988
Managed assets	39 802	38 158	36 047	34 032	29 918
Management fees	37,4	31,4	25,3	19,8	17,5
Administration fees as a percent of assets	0,094	0,082	0,070	0,058	0,058

Sources: Caisse de dépôt annual reports.

Some people would say that these management fees of under .1% are a bargain compared to the management fees of around .15% charged by the majority of the private management firms. But the private managers demand .15% fees on assets of an average of $500 million. We could expect much smaller administration fees from the Caisse de Dépôt considering its assets of $41 billion. In fact it should not be more costly to manage the $40-odd billion the Caisse had in 1992 than the $30-odd billion it managed four years earlier, in 1988. But then we have to take into consideration the natural tendency for a state agency like the Caisse de Dépôt to build itself into an empire. This does not seem to be an illogical conclusion when we see that the number of employees at the Caisse has increased from 195 in 1987 to 331 in 1992 — a rise of 70% in six years.

We can only hope that the provincial law which governs the operations and status of the Caisse be amended to permit a free choice of qualified Quebec-based managers for the public and para-public depositors (the free choice must obviously include the Caisse de Dépôt). These depositors are the nine institutions whose funds are by law, presently managed by the Caisse. Their acronyms are as follows: CARRA, RREGOP, SAAQ, CSST, CCQ, FAPAF, RMAAQ, RRTAQ and OPC.

If that amendment is not passed, another solution would be that the Caisse de Dépôt be divided in two. This would create a healthy competition in the management of our collective savings and a spirit of emulation, a welcome change from the existing monopoly of the Caisse in the management of our savings placed in the Régie des Rentes du Québec and in many other public and para-public funds. The two Caisses de Dépôt created from the division could still share the existing administrative structure which would in fact allow the managers of both agencies to lower their respective administrative fees. Each Caisse, with more than $21 billion in assets, would still be a significant player on the national and international scene and would find a renewed dynamism through the simple fact of motivated competition. Each Caisse would be able to attract new depositors either from private enterprise or from the other Caisse; after a few years the better of the two Caisses de dépôt would obviously have become bigger than the other, but the motor force of competition and emulation would remain.

By making sure that the Executive Officers of both these future savings management agencies are free from political influence, Quebecers could enjoy a much more fruitful and rational management of their savings.

CHAPTER II

State corporations, state capitalism?

THERE ARE A LARGE NUMBER of state corporations in Quebec. Many are relatively obscure, but the best known of them are also the ones that have siphoned off the most capital from the pockets of the province's taxpayers. My intention in this chapter is to discuss the state agencies in which I played a role — as a manager at the Caisse de Dépôt or as a member of the board.

ASBESTOS CORPORATION

When the Parti Québécois won the provincial election in November 1976, I had just been promoted to the position of Senior Corporate Investment Adviser at the Caisse de Dépôt. There was considerable concern on the investment committee of the Caisse — of which I was a member — regarding a particular electoral promise of the Parti Québécois. During the campaign the PQ had promised to transform Quebec into a kind of OPEC — the international oil cartel — with respect to our asbestos resources.

The Caisse de Dépôt at that time owned 5% of Asbestos Corporation — purchased at a cost of 21$ per share — and the managers had already heard an earful about the health and environment problems connected with asbestos fibers.

In fact, many lawsuits had already been instituted against asbestos users and producers, including the Johns-Manville company (the biggest North American asbestos producer) that was to go into receivership a few years later.

Several years earlier, the U.S. corporation General Dynamics of St. Louis had bought 51% of Asbestos Corporation at prices of about $20.00 per share. Sensing that the wolf might be at the door, the company had now began to cast around for a buyer of these shares.

The Parti Québécois's platform with its promise of an asbestos cartel was music to the ears of General Dynamics managers. Jacques Parizeau knew that it would have be a lot easier to gain control of a public corporation like Asbestos Corporation than to negotiate the purchase of 100% of Johns-Manville, which had the disadvantage of being both a private company and much bigger than Asbestos.

Parizeau — who became Minister of Finance in the Parti Québécois government — had concluded the public purchase offers to the electric utility companies for the creation of Hydro-Québec in the sixties. He saw a parallel in the negotiations with General Dynamics with a view to buying their controlling share of Asbestos Corporation and the takeover of private utilities by Hydro-Québec.

In a clever move, the Americans announced that their Asbestos Corporation shares were not for sale. Quebec's Premier René Lévesque then threatened a legislated nationalization.

During the time of this affair, around the month of May 1977, Marcel Cazavan — then president and general manager Caisse de Dépôt — arranged an appointment for me at the office of Jacques Parizeau, who as Finance Minister was the ultimate boss of the Caisse de Dépôt et Placement du Québec.

After cooling my heels — as protocol dictated — for at least half an hour, I was shown into Mr. Parizeau's office. I shook hands with the forty-three year old Minister of Finance in the Lévesque cabinet. As a preamble, I shared with him my worries about the consequences of the probable nationalization of Asbestos Corporation and the possibilities of lawsuits against the companies using and producing asbestos.

"Mr. Arbour, Mr. Parizeau answered, we are well aware of the lawsuits against Asbestos Corporation and General Dynamics (Asbestos Corp's majority shareholder). We are fully cognizant, he went on, of the problems that could result for the credit rating of the province of Quebec from the expropriation and the nationalization of Asbestos Corporation, but we will nonetheless take the necessary measures to honor the government's commitments."

I then asked him if the present government should be held to honor René Lévesque's electoral promise given that the nationalization costs could prove to be enormous. Mr. Parizeau answered that the electoral promise of Mr. Lévesque concerning asbestos was a solemn undertaking that Quebec's government would carry out and that the purchase, voluntary or not, of Asbestos Corporation would go through.

I had my misgivings upon leaving the meeting, and I informed the investment committee of the Caisse de Dépôt of what I had just learned.

To better situate these events in a historical context, it is worthwhile remembering that in 1977 Quebec's government considered the economic development of the asbestos-producing regions as one of the main components of its program of economic stimulus for the whole province. It was in the light of this policy that the provincial government founded, in May 1978, the Société Nationale de l'Amiante (S.N.A.) whose mandate was to purchase the asbestos companies as targeted by the law.

The first company targeted was Asbestos Corporation, owned, as previously mentioned, by General Dynamics of St. Louis. A first and reasonable offer of $42 per share had been rejected by the parent company. In 1979, to beef up the bargaining position of S.N.A., a law was adopted by the Quebec National Assembly, allowing the expropriation of Asbestos Corporation, if necessary.

To gain time, General Dynamics went to Quebec's Court of Appeal to challenge the power of expropriation as granted in this law. The company's suit was dismissed during the spring of 1981. Its patience then wearing thin, the provincial government set a deadline of November 30, 1981 for reaching a negotiated settlement, and the nationalization without expropriation finally took place.

A complicated arrangement allowed Quebec to delay the date of payment for the purchase of Asbestos Corporation. On November 9, 1981 the Société Nationale de l'Amiante bought the Asbestos Corporation shares held by General Dynamics, at a total cost of $165 million — an effective price of about $85 per share.

No corresponding offer was made to the minority shareholders, despite the obligation to do so under the rules of the Ontario Securities Commission, which regulatory body had jurisdiction on Asbestos Corporation inasmuch as the company was listed on the Toronto Stock Exchange.

For the first time in our history, an expropriation created the improbable situation where the foreign majority shareholder, American in this case, was very well paid, so as not to offend him. The local, minority shareholders got nothing.

This intolerable situation was quite naturally challenged in court. The Supreme Court of Canada eventually pronounced judgment in June 1993 in this suit. The Court asserted the right of the Ontario Securities Commission to oblige Quebec to make an offer — similar to the one obtained by General Dynamics — to the minority shareholders of Asbestos Corporation. If the Quebec government loses the case before the Ontario Securities Commission, the cost for the province will be very high indeed. Including interest, Quebec would have to pay a total amount of $130 million — a cost of about $120 per share.

In the meantime, the sales situation of asbestos fibers has kept on deteriorating. The low point was reached in July 1989 when the American government announced that it was blocking all asbestos imports in the Unites States.

Seeing no way out, Quebec's government — via the Société Nationale de l'Amiante — finally sold its interest in Asbestos Corporation in September 1992. The sale price was $34 million, payable over many years. The buyer, the Mazarin Group, was also guaranteed that the provincial government would be responsible of all lawsuits against Asbestos Corporation initiated prior to the purchase by Mazarin.

Here are the costs — as shown in Table VIII — of this adventure for Quebec's taxpayers. These costs do not include the legal fees and the considerable interest on the amounts involved.

**TABLE VIII
COST OF THE
ASBESTOS CORPORATION EXPROPRIATION**

(in millions of $)

November 1981, Purchase of General Dynamics shares	165
January 1986, Purchase of Bell Asbestos, Atlas-Turner and Lab Carysotile by S.N.A.	20
December 1990, S.N.A. long term loan	55
December 1991, Pension Fund Liability	2
SUB-TOTAL	242
LESS:	
Sale by S.N.A. (September 1992) (payable over 10 years)	(34)
Cost (before Supreme Court decision)	208
Additional probable cost, not counting legal costs, in case of an unfavorable decision by the Supreme Court	130
PROBABLE FINAL COST	**338**

THE QUÉBECAIR CASE

Around the middle of 1977 — after the election of the government of the Parti Québecois — a political decision was taken to create a number of new ministries. They were called "super" ministries because, in addition to their own direct sectoral responsibilities, they were each placed in charge of other ministries. Bernard Landry, the then-rising star of the Parti Québécois, was given a super ministry where he could allow his formidable energy to express itself. As a super Minister, Mr. Landry had considerable credibility in Cabinet and was in his own case the boss of Transport Minister Michel Clair.

I decided on March 3, 1978, to request an interview with Mr. Landry. He official title was State Minister for Economic Development. As for myself I was still an employee of the Caisse de Dépôt — with the impressive title of Senior corporate investment advisor.

I had previously met Bernard Landry at the end of the sixties when he was a young civil servant working for the Natural Resources Ministry. Minister Landry, sophisticated and self-confident, welcomed me in his office and immediately began talking about the economic orientation of Quebec.

I realized that Mr. Landry was very preoccupied with a dossier that was very much in the headlines at the time, concerning Québecair. I expressed my opinion that it seemed to me a wiser course that the Quebec government not get involved in this affair. The Minister smiled smartly and asked me, with

97

some irony, if businessmen still believed in the "invisible hand" of Adam Smith. This was a transparent reference to the fact that Quebec — in the person of its super Minister — had decided to dispense with the old concepts of the respective roles of private enterprise and the state and to act in this affair as a state entrepreneur.

Here were the essential facts: Alfred Hamel, a former trucker, had taken control of Québecair by buying — to applause by the current provincial political powers — the majority interest of the company held by Montreal financier Howard Webster. The aviation age had finally arrived in Quebec! For the first time a significant airline was owned by francophone interests.

Soon after his purchase, Mr. Hamel decided to seek partners to help him navigate successfully through the pitfalls of an industry that, albeit somewhat related to road transport, was one that he did not know well. Hamel succeeded in obtaining the financial help of other Quebec investors, including the Société d'Investissements Desjardins.

Some time later, in July 1981, Nordair of Montreal made a purchase offer to all Québecair shareholders for a total amount of $4.3 million (Nordair was then 82% owned by Air Canada, who was represented on the board by Jean Douville.). Nordair's offer for Québecair, by the way, was described as being financially "exemplary" by the Ministry of Bernard Landry.

Mr. Douville was not aware, however, that Mr. Hamel, the president and majority shareholder of Québecair, was in constant contact with Mr. Landry. In July 1981, after having unsuccessfully demanded from Nordair a modification of their offer to include certain personal privileges, Alfred Hamel initiated negotiations on the future of Québecair with the Quebec government.

Still in July of that year, a meeting was arranged between the interested parties, including Jean Douville (Vice-President of Air Canada), Roland Lefrançois (Chairman of the board of Nordair), and André Lizotte, President of Nordair. On that occasion, Bernard Landry announced to the President of Nordair that the Quebec government intended to counter Nordair's offer. The province would propose a slightly higher amount of $4.8 million — and promise an immediate investment of $15 million so as to improve Québecair's balance sheet which was not strong. During the same meeting Bernard Landry confided to Mr. Douville that one of his personal dreams was to one day land at Paris' Charles-de-Gaulle airport in an airplane bearing the fleur-de-lys on its tail. The government of Quebec would soon make the Minister's dream come true.

The provincial government paid Alfred Hamel almost $2 million for his Québecair shares. He even received a bonus which had been absent from Nordair's offer. But despite the new $15 million injection of capital, Québecair's balance sheet did not improve. Important airplane purchases — for $75 million — were made in 1982 in order to modernize the fleet. And it quickly became evident by the end of 1982 that Québecair needed an additional influx of $56 million just to be able to survive until the next year.

Landry, and transport Minister Michel Clair had neglected economic imperatives in order to advance nationalist and political considerations. Unfortunately, the situation continued to deteriorate at Québecair during the course of 1983. After the victory of the Liberal Party in the provincial elections of 1985, Québecair's dossier was handed to Fernand Lalonde, an attorney. He was given the thankless task of finding a solution to Québecair's ills so that the government could rid itself of this growing financial burden. Some time passed before finally, in July 1987, a consortium composed of Quebec businessmen and Canadian Pacific Airlines agreed to pay $10 million for the assets of Québecair, minus the accumulated deficit since the beginning of 1987. This came to a net amount of $5 million — the book value of the balance of the assets. According to Jean Douville, the former President of Nordair, this adventure had cost Quebec taxpayers the tidy sum of $120 million.

The sad story of Québecair came finally to an end in 1991, by the absorption of what was left of it by Canadian Airlines and the disappearance of the name Québecair — so loved by certain politicians.

THE S.G.F. GROUP
(Société Générale de Financement)

Mandate: "S.G.F. has the mandate to promote and carry out, in cooperation with other partners, industrial development projects in strategic areas of Quebec's economy in accordance with Quebec's economic development policies."[1]

This state corporation was the ancestor of all the other Quebec state corporations. Founded at the beginning of the sixties, it received an initial mandate of fostering industrial alliances and acquired 75% of Marine Industries. Later on, the corporation — after being privatized — made investments in publicly-held corporations like Domtar. This latter company, counting S.G.F.'s investment along with that of the Caisse de Dépôt, has in fact been placed under the direct control of the state.

Apart from Domtar, S.G.F.'s main investments are in the aluminum sector: Aluminerie Bécancour Inc. (25%) and Aluminerie Alouette Inc. (20%). S.G.F.'s financial interests in these two aluminum projects now amount to more than $585 million. When we add to this sum the investment of the Caisse de Dépôt in Alcan — more than $272 million as of December 31, 1992 — we can say that Quebecers have invested without knowing it a total of more than $857 million in three aluminum companies.

---

1   From the 1991 Annual Report.

Quebec's taxpayers should say a prayer every night for a recovery of the white metal's prices from the present low of $0.60 per pound, and for Russia to stop its international dumping of aluminum. Without that, S.G.F. will have to ask its shareholder (Quebec's government) to cover the unavoidable 1992-1993 losses resulting from aluminum sales below cost. Meanwhile, Hydro-Québec — which subsidizes the electricity used by the aluminium smelters — will also go on losing significant amounts of money in this activity.

The petrochemical industry is another sector in which S.G.F. is active. Because of international competition, this industry is also going through very lean years. As S.G.F. does not publish income statements by activity sector, it is almost impossible to estimate the losses generated by its investments in the petrochemical industry. In 1992 though, S.G.F. revealed that Ethylec — a 50%-owned subsidiary — had losses of $31 million and that Petromont, located in Montreal's east end, was still not performing well. The latter corporation is experiencing major difficulties even if both Canada's and Quebec's governments provided financial assistance of $50 million for the years 1983-1984. It also received $5 million in subsidies from Quebec for the year 1990 and $25 million in September 1993.

My own estimates of annual losses accruing to the S.G.F. from its petrochemical sector come to $35 million. The losses will go on as long as chemical products' prices do not recover in the international market.

Another very real nightmare for S.G.F. comes from the shipbuilding and naval sector represented by its subsidiary MIL Group Inc. — formerly Marine Industries Ltd. In the mid-eighties, this company obtained an important subcontract to construct frigates for the Canadian navy. Unfortunately for MIL, the execution of this contract has proven to be a financial bottomless pit. MIL — owned entirely by S.G.F. — is at present being sued for $1.7 billion by the general contractor of the frigates, who in turn is also being sued by S.G.F. for $20 million. The political powers soon stepped in to try and solve this untenable situation. At the end of 1991 they gave to the MIL Group financial assistance of $363 million — $263 million coming from the federal government and $100 million from the provincial government.

Finally, S.G.F. — along with the Caisse de Dépôt — bought over the years almost $28 million of Domtar shares at a cost, according to published financial statements, of $296 million. The market value of these shares being $146 million as of December 31, 1992 we can conclude that S.G.F. has suffered an unrealized capital loss of $150 million on this investment.

So the province, after having invested more than $350 million in S.G.F over the years, is now obliged to subsidize directly two divisions of this corporation — the petrochemical and shipbuilding sectors — and indirectly to subsidize the aluminum factories through Hydro-Québec's special deals on electricity . With S.G.F.'s long-term bank debt of more than $480 million as of December 31, 1992 and an unfavorable climate, it is a sure bet that S.G.F.'s shareholder will soon again be called upon to come with more cash, unless an unforeseeable buyer should appear on the scene and rid us of this white elephant. Now, I estimate at about $775 million Quebec's investment in S.G.F., including the financial help to the subsidiary companies in trouble. Clearly, the amount that could be raised by a sale to the private sector would be well short of that figure.

SIDBEC AND ITS SIDBEC-DOSCO SUBSIDIARY

Mandate: "To carry on the exploitation of a steel complex, alone or with partners, in order to insure, under conditions of profitability, the consolidation and expansion of its operations so as to stimulate in Quebec the development of industrial enterprises using steel."

The creation of Sidbec had its origin in a desire of Jacques Parizeau when he was special adviser to the Lesage government. Mr. Parizeau wanted to counterbalance steel prices that were higher in Quebec than in Ontario because of the absence of production in his province, mainly in flat steel. So Sidbec was created at the beginning of the sixties by the passage of a law.

In the middle of the sixties Sidbec bought the Dosco company. This company had just made its first important investment in Contrecoeur for a flat-rolled mill equipped with second-hand German machines. Unfortunately, this plant never succeeded in producing flat steel of a quality high enough and in quantities sufficient to satisfy its customers.

Sidbec operated with more or less uniform losses, making new investments at the same time. During the seventies the company invested in a steel reduction mill using a Swedish method, that seemed very promising.

Around that time, in 1977, the P.Q. government decided that Quebec should not have to depend any more on external sources for the purchase of iron ore. After all, the province had in its north significant deposits of that raw material. What was needed, apparently, was vertical integration that would enable Sidbec to retain profits connected to the production of iron pellets extracted from the iron ore and create jobs on Quebec's North Shore. The omnipresent Jacques Parizeau convinced then President of Sidbec, Jean-Paul Gignac, to undertake iron ore production by creating Sidbec-Normines.

A gigantic investment of almost $700 million was poured into Jeannine Lake in order to build a complete town and the necessary facilities for extracting and producing iron ore. The interest of Sidbec in this venture was 50% and the balance was divided between British Steel and U.S. Steel.

Unfortunately the whole world — including Brazil, Australia and certain Canadian competitors — could produce iron ore and iron pellets cheaper than Sidbec. There soon was an international overproduction that plunged the Jeannine Lake investment into the red, particularly around 1982. By 1984 Quebec's government let Sidbec know that it would no longer finance its deficit, and Sidbec had to close its mine in Jeannine Lake and dismantle all its facilities. Total cost of the venture: $343 million, financed with the help of a guaranty from the Quebec government. The province keeps the fiction alive by accepting each year in the National Assembly the filing of Sidbec's financial statements. The company has no assets, and a debt of $343 million financed by public funds.

After the write-off of that debt, Sidbec-Dosco was finally able to earn a profit after many very difficult years. Quebec's government was fully responsible for the loan Sidbec had taken for the Jeannine Lake investment and also for almost $50 million in total annual losses from 1977 to 1984.

On December 31, 1990 the government's investment in Sidbec was worth $233 million. This means that the province has invested about $1 billion in this company over the years. Curiously enough, at the beginning of May 1993, Sidbec was unable to produce its annual reports for 1991 and 1992. In June 1993 Sidbec finally declared a loss of $119 million for the year 1991. This loss wiped out the profits of the previous five years. According to reliable sources, losses for 1992 should be around $100 million. And Sidbec expects to experience losses again in 1993. This state corporation, by the way, has an unusual privilege: it is exempted from federal and provincial corporate income taxes. If one day Sidbec finally started to make a lot of money...

THE SOCIÉTÉ DE DÉVELOPPEMENT INDUSTRIEL DU QUÉBEC (S.D.I.)

Mandate: "To encourage the economic development of Quebec. Principal financial arm of the government in questions of economic intervention, the Société has taken part in the development and the modernization of a large part of Quebec's industrial structure."

This corporation — on the board of which I sat from 1976 to 1979 — basically takes over where the Federal Bank of Development stops. The S.D.I. accomplishes an enormous amount of company financing, and that work has increased due to the recession. Speaking very frankly, without the S.D.I. many Quebec corporations would now be bankrupt.

Finally — as detailed in the 1992 Annual Report — "the S.D.I. can intervene, on the government's demand, using loans, loans guarantees or capital stock purchases in order to contribute to the realization of major projects. This government mandate, given to S.D.I. according to article 7 of its charter, aims to answer the financial needs of projects deemed of strategic importance to the economic development of Quebec."

Under this article though, all loans of more than $1 million have to be approved by the provincial cabinet. This allows the politicians an important and direct say in the major decisions of this corporation. It should be remembered that the S.D.I. in 1989 gave a loan of $50 million to Steinberg and an even more important no-interest loan of $150 million to Domtar. In March 1992 this latter loan was converted into $150 million of preferred C shares.

By its very structure, the S.D.I. is subject to the decisions of provincial political power. The financial contributions of the provincial government to the S.D.I. over the years amply demonstrates that fact. According to the 1992 S.D.I. Annual Report, Quebec guarantees off-balance sheet loans contracted by S.D.I. customers to the tune of $764 million, $83 million in repayable contributions and $410 million in guaranteed investment, which comes to a total amount of $1257 million.

The long-term funded debt guaranteed by Quebec's government amounts to $789 million, government advances to $284 million and deferred income and endowment by Quebec's government to $46 million. The total of the government guarantees of all kinds amounts to $2376 million, and this does not include commitments as of March 31, 1992 of $133 million in various programs assisting in the financing of companies, $73 million in anticipated losses and $348 million in other government guarantees.

During the period when I was sitting on the S.D.I. board of directors — between 1976 and 1979 — there were so many files to deal with that we had to rely almost entirely on the business plans and the budget projections submitted by the mostly Small Business clientele because the analysts were completely over-whelmed by the abundance of dossiers. Since that time things have improved somewhat, but the 1989 recession has created an new excess of work for S.D.I.'s employees because a number of the old investments are in trouble.

That is the reason why S.D.I. uses more and more outside analysts to produce reports recommending or nixing financing: they have to lighten the work load burden of their own internal analysts. Now, since these outside advisers' fees are in fact paid by the companies seeking financing, it is most probable that there are few negative reports from these consultants recommanding financing to the S.D.I..

S.D.I.'s role is essential to Quebec's economy, but the extent of the political involvement and financial exposure of the provincial government is not suffi-ciently well known by the public, who in the end, foots the bill.

SOQUIP

Founded at the end of the sixties, SOQUIP (Société Québécoise d'Initiative Pétrolière) had an initial mandate to help Quebec become less dependent on oil imports. This state corporation's mission was to explore the provincial basins that could be potential sources of hydrocarbons.

SOQUIP was presided by Bernard Cloutier, an engineer who had worked in Paris for a multinational oil company. During the seventies and the eighties, SOQUIP attempted to evaluate the hydrocarbons potential of the St. Lawrence basin. The corporation has also evaluated the potential of Gaspé where there had been certain historical references of the presence of oil dating back to the discovery of Canada by Jacques Cartier.

Quebec's geology being very different from Alberta's, for example, these exploration projects for hydrocarbons all met with failure. Only one natural gas discovery, near St. Flavien (located northeast of Quebec City) was of commercial value, and even this was only thanks to the gas being sold to a local brick factory. Around the beginning of the eighties, the executive officers of SOQUIP convinced Quebec's government to divert a large part of the corporation's annual budget to exploration in Alberta. This location seemed a more intelligent use of the talents of an corporation employing engineers, geologists and geophysicists. During this time there were significant numbers of Quebecers taking the plane each week for Calgary, to supervise the SOQUIP drilling in Alberta. Eventually it was apparent that these efforts, directed from Quebec City, did not produce the expected results. A year later, in 1982, SOQUIP decided to enter into partnership with Sceptre Resources, by exchanging its oil and gas properties for about 10 million shares of Sceptre. The deal was concluded thanks to a coordinated effort between

SOQUIP and the Caisse de Dépôt. The Caisse owned in 1991 more than 15 million shares of Sceptre Resources which had been bought by the Campeau administration.

With an interest of more than 20% held by two Quebec state corporations, Sceptre Resources was now almost completely under Quebec government control, to the great displeasure of its president Richard Guzella. He resigned from his position at the end of 1991.

A series of purchases — done in part with the help of money borrowed by Sceptre Resources itself — put the company in a weak position to deal with the oil price fall and the interest rates hikes that came at the end of the eighties. During 1991 the corporation, burdened by its debts, had to restructure its obligations and reinforce its financial statement. SOQUIP's investment in Sceptre Resources was then worth only $9.2 million — compared to a cost of almost $52 million. The results of this financial reorganization were well received by the markets. Sceptre's new shares soared during the first months of 1993, diminishing the previous capital loss suffered by SOQUIP on this investment.

But this whole business was just another example of a how well-intentioned transactions by two Quebec state corporations resulted in a considerable loss. At the end of 1992, SOQUIP's investment in Sceptre Resources had created an unrealized loss of more than $42 million. The Caisse de Dépôt incurred an unrealized loss of approximately $70 million in the same venture. The price surge of Sceptre's shares at the beginning of 1993 will reduce this collective loss of $120 million to close to zero at the end of 1993.

The other important investment of SOQUIP is its 50% interest in Noverco. This corporation owns 100% of the shares of Gaz Métropolitain. The other 50% of Noverco is held by the Caisse de Dépôt even if this institution is ostensibly not allowed to own more than 30% of the shares of any one company. Once again we witness the coordination of government intervention, allowing two state agencies to own 100% of the shares of a private company.

The investment in Noverco proved to be profitable for SOQUIP which earns important revenues from it. Despite the recent profitability of the agency though, we have to remind ourselves that Quebec's government has sunk $214 million into SOQUIP. This amount does not include the grants for exploration on provincial territory given by the federal government from 1981 to 1986.

After more than 20 years of efforts, SOQUIP seems to have achieved three goals:

1. The discovery that there are no hydrocarbons in sufficient quantities for commercial exploitation in Quebec itself, hence the decision to go to Alberta to find some.

2. The takeover — with the Caisse de Dépôt — of the only natural gas distribution company in Québec, Gaz Métropolitain.

3. The difficult launching of the Soligaz project — in conjunction with the S.G.F. — that was to supply Quebec with liquid natural gas, allowing in this way the province to improve its competitive position on the North American markets. There will have to be more subsidies from the provincial government though to complete Soligaz. This enterprise is still high-risk and is strongly contested by the ecological movement. A terminal will have to be build in Varennes on the south shore of the St. Lawrence river to receive methane tankers. Soligaz will always be a high-risk operation and the target of much controversy. [2]

2   On June 17, 1993 Quebec Premier Robert Bourassa announced the indefinite suspension of the Soligaz project.

TABLE IX
ESTIMATED QUEBEC GOVERNMENT
FINANCIAL EXPOSURE
IN SELECTED STATE AGENCIES

(in millions of $)

	Grants and accumulated losses	Remaining Capital	Total exposure
S.N.A. (Asbestos)	338	0	338
Québecair	120	0	120
S.G.F.	175	600	775
Sidbec-Dosco	919	14	933
S.D.I. (*)	206	2409	2615
Soquip (**)	19	195	214
Total	1777	3218	4995

Source: Recent Annual Reports of above corporations.

(*) Note: This remaining capital is composed of $2376 million in loans and guarantees from the government of Quebec and the rest of the initial investment.

(**) Note: Figure does not count the federal subsidies accorded for petroleum exploration during the years 1981 to 1985.

114

THE PARAMUNICIPAL CORPORATIONS
OF THE CITY OF MONTREAL

Moved by a laudable desire of fostering economic development, the City of Montreal more than ten years ago created SODIM (Société de Développement Industriel de Montreal). This corporation joins three other paramunicipal agencies also operating in the local real estate sector: OMHM (Office Municipal d'-Habitation de Montreal), SHDM (Société d'-Habitation et de Développement de Montreal) and SIMPA (Société Immobilière du Patrimoine Architectural de Montreal). I will not analyse here two other Montreal's paramunicipal agencies — CIDEC and CIDEM — whose mandates are essentially social and cultural.

The four paramunicipal agencies operating in the real estate sector each have a board of directors and well-staffed executive offices, all of it under the responsibility of the president of the executive committee of the City of Montreal. SHDM, the most important agency, employs 229 people and has assets of $336 million; there are also long-term and bank loans of $291 million.

According to the last financial statements — dating from December 1992 — SDHM, with income of $37 million, has shown a small deficit despite a considerable amount of subsidies. These subsidies came from the City of Montreal, the Ministry of Culture of Quebec, the Canadian Housing and Mortgage Corporation, and finally, from the Société d'Habitation du Québec. For the year 1991, the subsidies totaled more than $25 million.

In 1991 SHDM bought the site of the Blue Bonnets racetrack from Campeau Corporation which was then in financial difficulty. The site is now rented to the Blue Bonnets Hippodrome for a nominal price in order to facilitate the activities of horse racing in Montreal.

But the situation of the Blue Bonnets racetrack is actually stagnant, in part because of the recession but also because of the precarious financial situation of SHDM. No real estate development has been started since 1991 on this huge piece of land (six million square feet) and there does not seem to be any real estate development currently planned on this location.

The purchase of Blue Bonnets could probably have been made by a private corporation without the money of the "poor" taxpayers of the City of Montreal. These taxpayers have involuntarily invested in this venture via the SHDM financing. Many people also think that there is favoritism shown the SHDM in the municipal evaluation of its properties — which would constitute a disguised subsidy.

As for SODIM, its administrative chart would delight students of any university business administration faculty. Not counting a board of directors of nine members, it includes an auditing committee, an executive committee and four departmental managers under the responsibility of a general manager. This agency had a permanent staff of 28 as of April 1993.

Today SODIM has loans payable of $75 million. A loss of $6.5 million for 1991 was followed by another one for 1992, this time of $8.6 million. According to the SODIM itself, the projected deficit for 1993 should be around $16 million. These figures do not include the special subsidies of the City of Montreal — via the PROCIM incentive program — that amounts to about $3 million per year. These subsidies are paid to tenants of properties owned by SODIM.

The impossibility of predicting the sharp drop in real estate values in 1989 — when most of these commitments were made — is the excuse generally given to explain that poor performance. This may indeed be so, but who is now saddled with this debt ? Who will invest in the renovation of the Nordelec building, an enormous historic eight-story building and former Northern Electric manufacturing facility bought by SODIM at the end of the eighties ? Who will pay for the demolition of the Redpath Industries building also bought around the same time and now in ruins ? Was it necessary to use taxpayers' money for a risky development to revive the neglected industrial Point St. Charles district in southwest Montreal? A direct incentive program and aid to the private sector to incite the renovation of this neglected industrial district might have possibly been more efficient. An exemption of municipal taxes for five to ten years could have gained the same results. That would have avoided the exposure of a paramunicipal agency on which it is very difficult to exert any financial control and which will still be the responsibility of the City of Montreal year after year.

Montreal's bureaucrats will someday have to examine all these questions. The citizens of the city are entitled to a comparative study of the cost-profit profiles of the paramunicipal agencies — including SODIM — compared to a scenario where the private sector would develop the neglected districts with the help of municipal tax exemptions.

As for SHDM and SIMPA, they are the happy owners — each with 18.75% — of the World Trade Centre opposite the Montreal Stock Exchange Building. This complex includes a luxury hotel, the Intercontinental. This ambitious real estate project is now open, but 40% empty. The initial private promoter had to sell his investment to the two paramunicipal agencies when he proved unable to assume his share of an $86 million refinancing for this center. Eventually, in 1993, both paramunicipals unloaded the loan to their own shareholder, ie the City of Montreal. The city had to itself borrow the required $86 million, relying on its taxation powers — thanks once more to the taxpayers. SHDM and SIMPA are in good company, by the way: the Caisse de Dépôt owns 45% of this real estate complex while the private sector — represented by Canada Life — holds a 17.50% share.

I evaluate at more than $120 million the financial involvement of the City of Montreal in these four paramunicipal agencies operating in the real estate sector. In addition, in order to ensure the survival of these agencies, annual subsidies of around $95 million are believed to be given by the City. Concerned citizens should open a serious public debate on the subject of the financing of these paramunicipal agencies.[3]

---

3   On June 15, 1993 the auditor of the City of Montreal deposited his annual report for the fiscal year ending on December 31, 1992. In this report, auditor Guy Lefebvre calls attention to the waste of many millions of dollars, the absence of controls and generalized laxism in many municipal programs and services. Mr. Lefebvre also notes that the purchase of the Blue Bonnets site by SHDM in 1991 was irregularly made without the prior consent of the Municipal Council of the City of Montreal.

TABLE X
ESTIMATED FINANCIAL EXPOSURE
OF THE CITY OF MONTREAL
IN FOUR PARAMUNICIPAL CORPORATIONS
(AS OF DECEMBER 31, 1992)

(in millions de $)

Org.	Assets	Loans	Capital and advances	Grants Montreal	Grants Quebec	Losses
SHDM	317	291	67	14*	5	13
SODIM	77	77	2	3	-	9
SIMPA	154	141	51	3	-	10(E)
OMHM	136	136	1	7	57	64**
	684	645	121	27	62	96

*Excludes an amount of $5.7 million from the Canadian Mortgage and Housing Corporation.

** These losses are balanced by grants in the same amount.

(E): Estimated

Sources: Most recent available Annual Reports

"Keep government out of business
and leave government
in the business of governing. "

(American proverb)

STATE CORPORATIONS, A CONCLUSION

We have shown that the governmental incursions into Quebec's economy using state corporations have often been spectacular failures. Despite the mitigated success of certain more modest state corporations — like SOQUEM for example that is probably the exception confirming the rule — the state does not even have sufficient resources to supply the necessary funds needed for the modernization and the expansion of the corporations owned by the province of Quebec. Just as bad, the state, by the nature of the political mechanisms that bring governments to power, cannot easily find or does not want to find the will to take draconian recovery measures made necessary by the current difficult economic times.

There is an important lesson to be learned from the interventionist adventure of Quebec's state corporations during the last thirty years. The state is made for governing, and not created to manage corporations, and while there was an undoubted laudable intention behind this activity, ie the politicians wanting to compensate for the collective absence of francophone Quebecers from the controls of economic power, this has unfortunately led to the transformation of the taxpayers of Quebec into involuntary shareholders. They are the ones who are now paying the costs of these adventures.

This economic interventionism — inspired by a French experience even more painful than ours — has distracted us and our resources from the vital priorities, so often stated, of education, health and infrastructure.

A serious effort to sell off the state agencies should be made, with the exception of the Société de Développement Industriel du Québec (S.D.I.). This would provide a way to create financial resources that could be used to diminish Quebec's debt or to improve the budget deficit of the province. Such a sale would block the temptation of any new financial engagements to help these agencies stay afloat.

My recommendation is even more pertinent in the case of the City of Montreal. The city is fighting a dramatic economic decline, while at the same time it invests huge sums of money in the above four paramunicipal agencies operating in the real estate sector. Lest the reader think that Quebec, or Montreal is special in this respect, my advice applies clearly to similar cases in the rest of Canada where the waltz of billions has also proceeded unabated. Foremost might be the Petro-Canada disaster which followed the National Energy Policy (N.E.P.) of 1980 and the misadventures, among others, of the provincially-owned companies BRIC in British Columbia, Novatel in Alberta, UTDC in Ontario and SYSCO in Nova Scotia.

APPENDIX

In the difficult budget context in which Quebec finds itself, Roland Parenteau — former Dean of the École National d'Administration Publique (ENAP) — recently made a startling announcement.[4] According to him, there are 6000 professionals too many employed by the Quebec government. The annual salary cost for these superfluous employees comes to approximately $300 million.

On the same subject, it is fascinating to count the number of governmental agencies that presently exist outside the ministries. There are 239 different agencies, operating under the responsibility of 29 ministers, including Quebec's premier. All of these agencies are required to have a board of directors, a chief executive officer, managers and support staff; these together represent a considerable expenditure of money. There are also the expenses incurred for their office rent and general administration.

Among these agencies I count 27 whose goals are the administration or the commercialization of goods and services. A large number of these 27 agencies could be privatized without causing any problems at all for the citizens and thus allowing Quebec to lower its budget deficit.

---

4   Le Devoir, May 13, 1993.

This book has only looked at only six (identified with an asterisk) of these state agencies; the list of the entire 27 follows in Table XI.

TABLE XI
GOVERNMENT-OWNED
PROFIT-SEEKING AGENCIES

1.   Hydro-Québec
2.   James Bay Development Corporation
3.* Société Nationale de l'Amiante
4.   Société Québécoise d'Exploitation Minière (SOQUEM)
5.* Société Québécoise d'Initiative Pétrolière (SOQUIP)
6.   Institut Armand-Frappier
7.* Sidbec
8.* Société de Développement Industrial du Québec (S.D.I.)
9.   Société des Alcools du Québec
10.* Société Générale de Financement du Québec (S.G.F.)
11. Société des Industries Culturelles
12. Société d'Habitation du Québec
13. Société immobilière du Québec
14. Société Parc-Auto du Québec Métropolitain
15. Société de Radio-Télévision du Québec
16.* Caisse de Dépôt et Placement du Québec
17. Société des Loteries du Québec

18. Société de Récupération, d'Exploitation et de Développement Forestier du Québec (REXFOR)[5]
19. Société du Port Ferroviaire de Baie-Comeau
20. Société des Traversiers du Québec
21. Office du Crédit Agricole du Québec
22. Société Québécoise d'Iniatives Agro-alimentaires (SOQUIA)
23. Corporation d'Hébergement du Québec
24. Société des Établissements de Plein Air du Québec
25. Régie des Installations Olympiques
26. Société du Palais des Congrès de Montreal
27. Société Québécoise des Pêches.

Source: Ministry of the Executive Council. May 14, 1993.

---

5   This corporation declared a loss of $75 million for 1992 that includes the expenses connected to the closing of a pulp factory in Port-Cartier, Quebec. This amount does not include the losses of the S.D.I. on loans of around $50 million or the subsidies given by Quebec to Rexfor.

CHAPTER III

The question of industrial grants

T HE PROVINCE OF QUEBEC is in practice obliged to offer grants, "sweeteners" to corporations who build new plants on its territory. Having vied with Ontario for quite a long time and more recently with the entire United States for the location of new industries, Quebec faces fierce competition in order to attract these investments, improve its economy, and keep up with the rest of North America. The total value of these subsidies, coming from the federal as well as from the provincial side, usually represents an important part of the investment decision. If you add to this the loans with subsidized interest rates, corporations which establish themselves in Quebec can recover up to a third of their investment in subsidies of all kinds. The large international corporations have really mastered the art of creating a bidding competition between different regions trying to attract their new plants. Unfortunately it is often the taxpayers, in this case Quebec taxpayers, who have to bear the burden of such a policy.

Now, the more unpopular any one region is with the industry looking for a new site, the higher will be the subsidies promised as compensation by industrial commissioners. As for municipalities, not only do they grant these corporations municipal tax refunds, they also sell them land at very cheap prices.

How can we diminish the subsidies required to attract the establishment of new industries ? To answer that question, we must first divide these investment decisions into two categories : those made by local companies and those made by international companies controlled most of the time by foreign capital.

In Quebec, the local companies are mainly composed of small and medium sized businesses that know the province well and have their roots here. The amounts of subsidies granted to these companies are quite modest, especially compared to the subsidies required by the larger corporations — often international ones — of the second category. This category exacts in fact the lion's share of the total amount of the subsidies, as the most important dollar share of investments made in Quebec comes from the large international corporations, mostly American. This despite the desire of our politicians who really want local small and medium-sized industry to assume a larger share of these investments.

How to attract these international American corporations without being obliged to subsidize an unreasonable part of their investments with our taxes?

Around the end of the sixties, the well known American magazine *Fortune* published a complex study made from a survey of the 500 largest American corporations indicating reasons that would motivate their choice of a particular area for the location of a factory.

Fifteen factors were given, the most evident being the proximity of markets, the presence of a modern transportation infrastructure, an educated and skilled labor force, etc. All these factors collectively were important in the investment decision, but the most important one was the following, as quoted in *Fortune's* study : "Suitability of location for executives and their families". This human factor was the most important one of the "material" factors tending to influence the American decision makers; it is doubtless of equal importance to Canadian and European decision makers as well.

We have to remember this important factor when we try to attract capital to Quebec, and particularly to the Montreal area. The negative perception and publicity generated by the introduction of Quebec's language laws have more than cancelled the efforts made by the province to attract foreign industries. (See chapter VI entitled "Quebec Inc. and linguistic interventionism".)

HYDRO-QUÉBEC AND ITS INDUSTRIAL SUBSIDIES

During the years following the nationalization of the private electricity utilities in 1962, Hydro-Québec has become a colossus, thanks to its huge projects in the James Bay area. The corporation prided itself on having achieving a cost of electricity generation that was among the lowest in North America. A new mission was created in the eighties for Hydro-Québec : on top of producing electricity cheaply for its own population, it was now to become an industrial promoter.

This mission consisted of signing discount contracts with big users of electricity on the condition they build their new factories in the province of Quebec. This new strategy seemed brilliant, based as it was on the theory that massive contractual exports of our electricity to the United States brought less economic development than the building of new factories. At the begining of the eighties, Hydro-Québec made long-term deals with a number of corporations. These deals stipulated that the client corporations could buy electricity at minimal costs, periodically and proportionally adjusted to the market price of the finished product — in this case, aluminum and magnesium.

Two subsequent, unforeseen events though, became factors in derailing that strategy :

1. An American competitor of Norsk Hydro (one of the beneficiaries of this special deal) complained that Norsk obtained electricity at subsidized prices. The information concerning these preferential tariffs was contained in the secret contracts disclosed in 1992 by Robert Libman, a Quebec National Assembly Member and leader of the Equality Party. The

American Department of Commerce decided as a result to impose a compensatory anti-dumping tariff of 80% — later lowered to 38.94% — on all magnesium imports from Quebec.

2. Aluminum and magnesium prices have fallen more than 35% between 1985 and 1992. This prevented Hydro-Québec from raising its tariffs as set out in the adjustment clauses in the risk-sharing contracts.

At the end of 1992 Hydro-Québec had signed a known total of thirteen secret contracts selling electricity at discounted prices of $0.015 per kilowatt-hour against a cost for Hydro-Québec of $0.024 per kilowatt-hour. During that period, the regular tariff for a big user was $0.032 per kilowatt-hour, more than twice as much.[1]

We have learned from well-informed sources that it is possible that Hydro-Québec will sustain a net loss of around $3 billion from 1987 to 2010 if the prices of these metals do not regain their normal level in proportion with Canadian inflation rates. The current price of aluminium, at $0.60 per pound, is much lower than the break-even price in the secret contract. The price of this metal would in fact have to rise to more than $1.00 per pound for Hydro-Québec to stop subsidizing the aluminium producers.[2]

1   The Gazette, March 20, 1993.
2   Le Devoir, April 1, 1993.

We have to ask ourselves if the role of Hydro-Québec should really be to give subsidies, selling electricity at a discount in order to attract industries such as aluminum smelters that use large quantities of power. The province of Quebec runs the risk of raising the hackles of American competitors who have the power — and freely use it — to complain to U.S. authorities in a wide range of ways, which can and has resulted in penalties, punitive tariffs on exports to the United States that completely nullify the original subsidies. And again I ask, who foots the bill?

CHAPTER IV

Tax shelters

ONE OF THE MOST VIRULENT and chronic criticisms made by certain union leaders concerns the injustice of our tax system. For them, the fiscal advantages granted to investors result in enormous revenue losses for the Quebec government and consequent prejudice to the interests of low-income citizens. We will try to clarify this question and see if that declaration is reasonable.

THE QUEBEC STOCK SAVINGS PLAN

In 1978 Jacques Parizeau — then Quebec Minister of Finance — wanted to accelerate the industrial development of the province. He decided to create the Régime d'Épargnes Actions (R.E.A.) or Quebec Stock Savings Plan, which offered important deductions (from 75% to 150% on the Quebec portion of Income Tax) for certain types of investments. The avowed purpose was to foster access to capital for local companies, turn Quebecers into a nation of small shareholders, etc. Provincial income tax deductions were offered when individuals invested in so-called "Quebec" corporations — including Bell Telephone(!) and Consolidated-Bathurst (a 75% deduction) or Ogivar and Pro-Optic (150% deduction). The latter were both small companies that in fact no longer exist.

As the years want by, it was realized that companies like Bell Telephone did not really need the QSSP to obtain capital, but if an income tax deduction opportunity was given to individuals for investing in Bell or in Consolidated-Bathurst, many would avail themselves of it. This fiscal advantage was scaled down around 1988, dropping from 75% to 25% for big corporations, which lessened the excess of fiscal generosity for the industry.

As for the smaller, higher-risk corporations, most of them would never have obtained public financing without the presence of the QSSP, and the majority of these corporations have since taken a nose dive — at least as far as their share price and their financial stability are concerned. Most of these companies whose stock issue was promoted to small investors have come to an abrupt end. The process, though, did churn out considerable gains for the stockbrokers and their numerous consultants.

Some smaller companies were financially sound and profited in a better way from the QSSP program. There were a number of shares issued at high prices that generated capital under conditions more advantageous to the issuer than would have been the case in the absence of the plan. But this system's built-in tax incentive to investors also allowed shares to be floated and bought at exorbitant prices. The owners of the new shares received a tax break, but had to wait many years before being finally able to recover their initial investment.

In 1979 — before I left the Caisse de Dépôt — Jacques Parizeau explained to me his philosophy concerning QSSP. "We allow in this way a great number of small companies to come into existence and to obtain capital. Corporations in Quebec have always borrowed too much compared to corporations in Ontario. The QSSP will re-establish the balance and improve these corporations' financial statements."

Finally he added this surprising declaration :"The high-income wage earners) pay 10% more in combined personal federal and provincial income taxes in Quebec than in Ontario. They have only to invest each year the allowed QSSP maximum if they want to obtain the same net level of taxation as obtains in Ontario."[1]

This typical declaration "à la Parizeau" illustrates his lack of consideration for Quebec's taxpayers. He was quite ready to force them to use their savings to make investments that were at the least very speculative, in order to avoid paying excessive levels of provincial income taxes. He would probably never have had the idea to lower the personal income tax to the level of the Ontario one and to give at the same time a modest income tax deduction for investments

1   From 1982 to 1985 the difference between the income tax rates of Quebec and Ontario increased compared to 1979 to reach more than 20% (See Table XVIII).

in small corporations as an incentive for the public not to invest only to save on income tax. When we combine the 150% deductions of the QSSP with the investment in an R.R.S.P. (Registered Retirement Savings Plan), a taxpayer investing in one of the eligible corporations could reduce the real cost of his investment to practically nothing, thanks in large part to Revenue Québec and to Revenue Canada for the rest.

But does this policy really foster the development of intelligent long-term investing? Most of the small corporations that have profited from the QSSP do not exist any more. Many analysts — including Hubert Marleau, President of Marleau Lemire Inc. — now affirm that the corporations still in business would have been able to finance themselves without the help of the QSSP. We can say that clearly, the whole plan resulted in 1)loss of income tax revenue for the provincial government and 2)loss of capital for many small investors.

Table XII shows the amounts invested in the QSSP since its creation and the cost in lost revenue for the Quebec government.

TABLE XII
COMPILATION OF THE PRINCIPAL FIGURES
RELATIVE TO THE QUEBEC STOCK SAVINGS PLAN

1. From 1979 to 1985

(in millions of $)

	1979	1980	1981	1982	1983	1984	1985	TOTAL
Value of investments	109	150	248	214	766	716	1 273	3 476
Cost of plan to the State	15	31	36	53	145	160	194	634

2. From 1986 to 1992

(in millions of $)

	1986	1987	1988	1989	1990	1991	1992	TOTAL
Value of investments	1 746	553	403	167	275	241	735	4 120
Cost of plan to the State	127	50	30	12	13	40	91	363

TOTAL 1979-1992

Value of investments	7 596
Cost of plan to the State	997

Source: Quebec securities commission

136

We can see by the above that the cost of the Quebec Stock Savings Plan for the Quebec state has been about $1 billion since its creation. Has that loss been compensated by other revenue-producing economic activity ? Would it not have been more productive for the government to lower the marginal rate of Quebec income tax — which was at more than 67% between 1978 and 1981 — in order to attract capital funds ? I believe the reader can arrive at his or her own conclusions!

THE FILM INDUSTRY WRITE-OFF

It is probable that certain well-known financial scandals connected with the film industry were predestined. They certainly do not come as a surprise when you know the great latitude given to the promoters of these fiscal shelters. The complexity inherent to the motion picture industry also makes it extremely difficult to maintain a tight control of the contracted fiscal expenses. The ways and customs of this industry make it possible to achieve non profitability even for a blockbuster film because the expenses for management, marketing and advertising seem somehow to increase in proportion to gross revenues.

In Canada, on top of the generous fiscal deductions granted (100% of the investments), it is possible to increase an investment in the sector of cinematographic production thanks to loans guaranteed by advance sales. Fiscal deductions could then reach more than 200% and this gives investors a positive return arising solely from fiscality. Finally, there is a federal organization that is permitted to finance films through the means of loans and equity participation.

The taxpayers pay dearly for the desire of our politicians to help the movie industry in Quebec and the rest of Canada and counter the massive American film production. Nevertheless, it is true to say that Quebec was at least able to distinguish itself with a unique film voice, perhaps a somewhat more inventive voice than English Canada's that tried more to imitate Hollywood's most commercial aspects.

Meanwhile, an important part (from 20% to 25%) of the amounts obtained by public issues of film tax shelters are used for legal or administrative fees and for the payments of commissions. These fees profit a small group of privileged people who do not, in fact, have much to do with the cinema industry itself.

It seems to be virtually impossible to eliminate this fiscal shelter because it is so essential for film producers and it provides incomes for a lot of people who would otherwise be unemployed. But it would seem to me vital to develop some better controls to ensure that invested capital be allocated in the proper way by the film promoters.

TABLE XIII
TAX SHELTER INVESTMENTS, CINEMATOGRAPHIC
AND VIDEO PRODUCTIONS SECTOR

1986 to 1991

GROSS PROCEEDS FROM QUEBEC RESIDENTS

(in millions of $)

1986	1987	1988	1989	1990	1991	TOTAL
53	92	151	205	141	36	678

Source: Commission des valeurs mobilières du Québec

The fiscal deductions obtained represent 100% of the gross proceeds of $678 million.

FLOW-THROUGH SHARES

Flow-through shares are a relatively recent invention, dating from 1983. This system allows mining companies to offer private investors the advantages of the extremely generous fiscal deductions granted to companies doing mining exploration.

These income tax deductions — 166,33% for the Quebec portion and 100% for the federal share — mean that the taxpayers subjected to a tax rate of 50% enjoy almost a risk-free investment. The yield from the income tax deduction and the resale of their shares, even at low prices, allows them a sure profit on their total investment.

The enormous amounts of money invested by the taxpayers — and consequently by the state — have brought the discovery of a few mineral deposits, the best known being probably the Louvicourt mining project operated by Aur Resources of Toronto. But the exploration programs have not really yielded enough commercial discoveries. Without the incentive program, a mineral exploration project would in fact cost at least 30% less. In this sector, as in many others, costs often increase in proportion to the fiscal benefits granted.

A simple auditing system would be of great help in eliminating the most common abuses. For example, drilling contracts are often awarded to companies connected with the shareholders of the issuers. Also, administrations costs are exaggerated with the help of invoices from management corporations affiliated with the promoter. I am convinced that mineral exploration can be encouraged while avoiding at the same time the most flagrant abuses.

TABLE XIV
FINANCING OF THE MINING INDUSTRY OF QUEBEC
(FLOW-THROUGH SHARES)

(in millions of $)

1983	1984	1985	1986	1987	1988	1990	1991	1991	1992	TOTAL
43	65	157	288	532	154	73	44	9	18	1 383

Source: Ministry of Energy and Resources

These various financing operations over the past ten years have created for investors deductions of around $2 billion in provincial and federal income taxes.

But the big winners of this plethora of fiscal shelters — QSSP tax deductions, film and mining investment write-offs — are not always the investors, even less the taxpayers but instead the army of promoters, stockbrokers and fiscal advisers needed for the creation and management of these shelters.

CHAPTER V

The abuse of the system

NON-VOTING SHARES

A N IMPORTANT MEMBER of Quebec Inc., Serge Saucier — now President of a chartered accounting firm and also Chairman of the board of the École des Hautes Études Commerciales — was tasked in 1984 to formulate recommendations on the capitalization of companies in Quebec.

His report — later called the Saucier Report — was a document remarkable in its precision. It recommended to the provincial government a certain number of measures to help in the financing of corporations, but it was a missed opportunity as far as the attempt to correct one of the glaring weaknesses of our capitalization structure was concerned. I am talking about the existence of various categories of common shares. Our system allows many corporations to have a small number of voting B common shares kept in a few hands, often those of the founding shareholders and their families, while the investing public obtains for its money mostly A common shares with minimal or no voting rights attached (a 10% proportion of the votes given to A shares as opposed to B shares is common). A meaningful improvement though, has been given to holders of non-voting shares, as far as value is concerned, since these shareholders now have to get the same price granted to the voting shares when there is a sale of the company by the principal shareholder (the coat-tail provision). This new clause, unfortunately, is not retroactive; older corporations are exempted.

There are a number of older corporations with a background of more than 25 years on the Montreal Stock Exchange whose capital was already divided into two or more classes of common shares. One of the best known of these is Power Corporation where founder's common shares possessed ten votes per share compared to only one vote per share for other common shares. This allowed Paul Desmarais in 1968 to buy 51% of the votes of Power Corporation for an amount equal to hardly more than 10% of the company's capitalization.

Two other public corporations where flagrant abuse has been evident are Papiers Rolland Ltd. and Steinberg Inc. Both had non-voting class A common shares and voting common shares. In August 1989 Socanav bought the total existing number of non-voting class A shares and voting common shares. Socanav was forced to pay the Steinberg sisters — who held the majority of the voting common shares of the company built up by their father Sam Steinberg — a bonus of 47% compared to the amount of $51 per share offered to the public, i.e. $75 per common share. This difference — an additional cost of $144 million — was one the main reasons why

Michel Gaucher of Socanav was not able to make Steinberg profitable. Eventually this lack of profitability would bring about the liquidation of the company.

The most remarkable abuse though, occurred during the purchase by Cascades Inc. — one of the "flowers" of Quebec industry — of the non-voting common shares of Papiers Rolland as well as an important part of its voting shares. Cascades had in 1989 offered Papiers Rolland a very generous price of $20 per non-voting A share and $21 per voting B share.

Unfortunately for the Lemaire brothers, majority shareholders of Cascades, Lucien Rolland was not interested in their offer. This well-known executive — who held more than 51% of the shares of his company — refused to sell his voting common shares, and that let the offer for the A shares lapse. For more than two years, we witnessed the bizarre situation where the owner of almost 50% of the voting shares of a large corporation was frustrated and made powerless by the obstinacy of one man.

Finally at the end of 1992, Cascades capitulated and paid a bonus of 400% — compared to the price of the A shares that were then quoted at $5 on the stock exchange — for the voting B shares of Lucien Rolland, and that came to $21 per share.

Once more the controlling shareholder had obtained a high price for his shares. In the meantime, minority shareholders would probably have to wait a very long time indeed before seeing the market value of the A shares rise again to the $20 initially offered by Cascades.

After looking at these two extreme examples, let us examine the more common situation of some corporations registered on the Montreal Stock Exchange that were influenced by the Saucier Report. These corporations — Quebecor, G.T.C., Trans-Continental, Bombardier among the most important — all have A shares with 10% of the votes of the voting B shares. But they have a coat-tail provision which gives to the A shares the same price that the voting B shares would fetch in a sale when control of the company changes hands.

Nevertheless there is nothing to protect the minority shareholder from the consequences of the refusal of the controlling shareholder to accept a reasonable offer from a third party. We can anticipate a scenario where the obstinacy of a control shareholder would prevent the orderly transfer of a once dynamic corporation to a new group wanting to make a global purchase of the shares at a price quite favourable for the interests of the non-voting shareholders.

The *ipso facto* acceptance of A and B shares in the light of the Saucier Report and the benediction of the ruling securities commissions will, I believe, create a transfer of power problem that will make itself felt many years from now. The dynamic entrepreneurs of today, will, in the course of ageing, quite possibly become stubborn authoritarians who will refuse to relinquish their vote and their power to a younger generation of managers.

Certain more enlightened stockbrokers or investment dealers in fact now are loath to arrange financing for companies with more than one class of common shares. This system is particular to Quebec where practically all the companies controlled here have two classes of common shares. This problem does not exist in United States — where it is almost impossible to be listed on the New York Stock Exchange while having two classes of shares — and in English Canada — where two classes of shares are quite rare. The problems arising from the two classes of shares will, as I said above, manifest themselves far down the line. And the financial community will not be able to do a much to help the minority shareholder, deprived of voting rights on his common shares or having only 10% of the voting power of the founder's common shares.

BOARDS OF DIRECTORS AND BILL S-31

Democracy is the fashion nowadays. Hardly a day passes without self-congratulatory remarks being made about how lucky we are to be living in a democratic country instead of those countries of Eastern Europe or the Third World that are still very far from democratic rule.

The capitalist system has had for a long time a mechanism — democratic in appearance — to elect corporate directors, including the president and the chief executive officers. How are directors chosen ?

Most of the time by the president and chief executive officer who naturally wants to be supported by reliable people with experience in the industry but not necessarily in a sector connected to the one in which the corporation operates. Nevertheless there is a strong temptation to name to the board friends and relations who will not dare to contradict the chief executive officer — who is also chairman of the board. Gradually, and this is especially true if the corporation is an important one, the number of directors inexorably increases. It often exceeds forty persons, as is the case for the large chartered banks.

We have here two different problems. Firstly, how to choose the president and chief executive officer who will have to report to the board of directors ? Secondly, how to make the choice of the directors constituting that board?

Currently, shareholders elect the board of directors recommended by the chairman of the board who is usually also chief executive officer. If the stock is divided into non-voting class A shares and voting class B shares, there will not be much opposition to the list of directors presented to shareholders for approbation at the annual meeting of the corporation. Is it possible to create a mechanism that would allow shareholders, and especially institutional shareholders, to influence the corporation's general management which has in fact to report to the shareholders of that corporation ?

In the past, most corporations, even the important ones, combined the positions of president and chief executive officer in one person. Many corporations from both sides of the Atlantic have now started to separate these two positions, despite the opposition of many heads of companies who prefer the principle of only one "boss".

But we want that "boss" to be answerable to the shareholders. The ideal mechanism is to nominate a respected director who can accomplish the task of chairman of the board and be able to communicate shareholders concerns to the chief executive officer before, not after the advent of a disaster, for example.

As for the size of the board of directors, it has been stated by William E.F. Turner, former President and chief executive officer of Consolidated-Bathurst and present Chairman of the board of Canadian Marconi, that it is very difficult to have constructive discussions around a board of directors' table when there are more than twelve people attending. I concur with this evaluation as to the optimum number of directors. More than that number precludes any real possibility for the directors to make themselves heard and especially to have an opportunity to oppose certain projects presented by the executive offices. The boards that have the largest number of directors in this country are, as already mentioned, those of the big chartered banks. These directors, often close to forty in number, did certainly not have the opportunity nor the time during the meetings of their board to examine in depth the massive loans granted to speculative real estate promoters during the eighties, loans which so very quickly had to be written off as the real estate market crashed, thus leaving shareholders and taxpayers alike poorer.

To compensate for this internal loss of efficiency, an executive committee is sometimes created — especially in large corporations. The committee members are most of the time the President, the chief executive officer and three other external directors. The committee makes the important decisions and then presents them to the board of directors for final approval. It is very rare to see a board of directors oppose recommendations made by an executive committee whose members are colleagues who also sit on the board. That is why the boards of directors of most of our large publicly held corporations only have a distant role as advisers and are often used by the executive offices only to rubber-stamp their decisions.

Moreover, as most publicly held corporations of Quebec Inc. have a capitalization composed of non-voting (or less-voting) class A shares held by the public and voting class B shares held by the President and chief executive officer who presides the board of directors, it is easy to understand that it can be extremely difficult for one or even several members of the board to oppose projects proposed and supported by the main shareholder having a preponderance of voting rights.

Currently, the ownership of our corporations, whether they be from Quebec or the rest of Canada, is more and more in the hands of institutional capital — i.e. the people who manage our pension plans, insurance premiums, etc. It would seem to be only appropriate that corporations take into consideration the opinions of institutional shareholders who in fact represent the collective opinion of the contributors to their funds.

Around the middle of the seventies, the Caisse de Dépôt et placement du Québec engaged in a laudable effort of communication with the executive offices of the large corporations in which the Caisse had a position. The mechanism used was negotiations with these corporations in order to obtain direct representation on the board of directors, but the procedure did not always give results because there was a lot of distrust of the Caisse, especially after it became more political following the nomination of Jean Campeau as its President. The distrust increased when it became evident that the Caisse de Dépôt often departed from its role of fund manager into one of financial conglomerate *à la* Power Corporation.

On this subject, a comical incident that took place at the beginning of Mr. Campeau's tenure is worth mentioning. The Canadian financial community had an attack of paranoiac panic when the Caisse de Dépôt holdings of Canadian Pacific common shares reached the magic threshold of 9.9%. This huge Canadian conglomerate owned interests in almost all the economic sectors of the country. At the same time, Paul Desmarais of Power Corporation — with an ownership of 11% in C.P. — had begun negotiations with Jean Campeau in order to coordinate the actions of Power Corporation and the Caisse de Dépôt for a possible takeover attempt.

Just prior to these events — in 1980 — the Caisse de Dépôt had let it be known that it wanted a seat on the board of directors of C.P. Despite being rebuffed in this request, the Caisse decided to buy more Canadian Pacific stock, striking terror into the hearts of our fellow Canadians in the anglophone establishment.

Using all their political clout in Ottawa, they succeeded in having a bill introduced in the Canadian Parliament. This most unusual bill — S-31 — prevented the Caisse de Dépôt from buying more than 9.9% of Canadian Pacific shares. Despite Quebecers' protests against such partisan legislation — the protesters quite correctly saw it as an unacceptable protectionist reaction of English Canada toward Quebec — the bill introduced on November 2, 1982 has effectively blocked the Caisse's designs on Canadian Pacific. And to the great dismay of Jean Campeau, his ally Paul Desmarais, owner through Power Corporation of 11% of C.P. shares, declared himself on November 23, 1982 to be in favour of Bill S-31. Jacques Parizeau was livid, calling this about-face by Desmarais "aberrant" (Parizeau's recent call on Desmarais to sell his Montreal daily newspaper

La Presse to more "loyal" interests shows that the Parti Québécois leader has a long memory.[1]).

So the Caisse de Dépôt was obliged to abandon its designs on C.P. But in fact, without knowing it, the federal government had just saved the Caisse from making another disastrous transaction. The following years were full of reverses for Canadian Pacific and its shares fell considerably in market value. Not long after — in 1987 — the potential ally of the Caisse, Power Corporation, decided to sell its important position in C.P. and that put a full stop to this adventure.

CORPORATE GOVERNANCE

For the institutional capital fund managers who invest our savings, good management of corporations is a very legitimate concern in the best of times, and even more so when some firms are in dire straits as is unfortunately the case for many of our large Canadian corporations since the beginning of the recession in 1989.

There is still no mechanism which allows for shareholder input in the big corporations, except for the annual assembly that often is nothing more or less than an exercise in public relations. That is why we argue that external directors (i.e. those who are not employed by the corporation) are important

1   As reported by Jean-Claude Leclerc, The Gazette, October 25, 1993.

vehicles to defend unpopular points of view, with the caveat that these external directors not sit on too many boards because this dispersal of focus would prevent them from accomplishing valuable work. These corporation directors should be obliged to state annually the names of all their directorships, and this list should be made available to all shareholders of publicly-held corporations of which they are directors.

It would be advisable also to reduce the size of the boards of directors of publicly-held corporations to around twelve. This would eliminate the need for an executive committee and oblige instead more frequent meetings of the board, thus allowing a more intense involvement of directors in the affairs of the company. The composition of the board of directors should give a majority to the external members. This would avoid the inevitable sclerosis resulting from a situation when a corporate board is composed in majority of members reporting to the executive suite. Finally, in publicly-held corporations with sales of more than $1 billion, there should be two persons sharing the responsibilities of president and chief executive officer, not one person cumulating both positions. This would make these corporations more open to their shareholders' ideas and needs.

THE REMUNERATION OF EXECUTIVE OFFICERS

It is quite normal that the executive officers of a public corporation should be well paid. It is unacceptable though to hide the details of their individual remuneration from the shareholders by revealing only the global remuneration of the executive officers — the five to ten employees at the head of a publicly-held corporation.

It is aberrant that, in order to know the amount of the remuneration of Canadian Pacific's President, you have to communicate with the American Securities and Exchange Commission to get this information that is public knowledge in the United States. Canadian Pacific owning interests in United States, the corporation is obliged to conform to the disclosure rule of that country. This rule however does not apply in Canada due to the lobby of the large corporations, probably embarrassed to reveal to their trade unions the salaries of their chief executive officers. Mandatory in the United States, this obligation in the name of fiduciary transparency is so far absent from the playing field in Quebec and Ontario, although the Ontario Securities Commission has proposed disclosure requirements similar to those of the S.E.C.. A change à l'américaine of this procedure will evidently have to be coordinated between Quebec and the rest of Canada or it may create an exodus from one stock exchange to another. A recent proposition of the Montreal Stock Exchange on this subject has also been submitted to the Canadian regulatory organizations. According to this proposition, publicly-held corporations would have to reveal the salary of their President when it exceeds by 40% the salary of his principal assistant. This is a step in the right direction...but more steps are needed and inevitable.

STOCK OPTIONS

Included also in the remuneration of the executive officers of corporations are the stock options often granted in large number and at discount prices compared to the stock exchange share prices obtaining at the time the options are granted.

After considerable debate, it seems to be a real possibility that the Securities and Exchange Commission and the American Institute of Chartered accountants will adopt new rules governing stock options. When we learn that the President of Walt Disney or the President of Coca-Cola earned in 1992 sums exceeding $50 million, these huge amounts do not stem evidently from their salaries but come mostly from their participation in stock option plans granted them years earlier. The stock exchange accomplished wonders for some corporation CEOs. However, the stock option system brings with it an inevitable dilution of the assets of the existing shareholders. If Mr. Eisner, the President of Walt Disney, is allowed to buy 1 million shares of Disney at $10 per share while these shares sell for $42 at the stock exchange, the value of the shares held by the other investors diminish. Also, it is customary to offer a generous discount on the price of the stock options as an inducement to accept an important company position or to retain the services of a popular and efficient executive.

This discount can be as much as 15% of the initial price of the shares as listed on the Stock Exchange, and the option comes with the added privilege of being able to wait from five to ten years before it expires. This privilege is evidently not available to ordinary shareholders and it is more and more being openly suggested that the discount on stock options be abolished because it creates once again a dilution of the assets of the shareholders without corresponding benefit.

It would also seem appropriate that the Montreal Stock Exchange, the Quebec Securities Commission and the Institute of Chartered Accountants should study the desirability of adopting standards that would take into consideration the real accounting costs of the granting of stock options for publicly-held corporations.

Finally, the regulatory bodies could examine the problem of stock options granted at prices below market value. This a practise that in my opinion clearly abuses the rights of the other shareholders.

The candidate that a publicly-held corporation wants to attract as its President should expect an increase in value of the shares of his corporation only from the price on the stock exchange as of the date of his employment. Later on, he could rightly cash in on the stock-market results of his efforts.

BUREAUCRATIC ABUSE

Practically each and every entrepreneur who has started his or her own company can eloquently testify to the fact that a large part of their time is devoted to filling in forms from numerous governmental agencies. This obligation adds considerably to the administrative costs of a company. The larger companies can evidently deal with this problem by hiring employees whose sole tasks are to fill in those forms in order to comply with the requirements of the different ministries. The smaller companies though are often greatly penalized by the loss of time in responding to bureaucratic requirements — particularly those concerning wages of the employees.

I want to talk also about an evident bureaucratic abuse, an especially flagrant one, unique to Quebec, that exists nowhere else in North America. It is the abuse created by the Collective bargaining decrees. These decrees, legislated into existence in 1937 during the Great Depression, first led to the Law on Reasonable Salaries and more recently to the Law on Collective Bargaining Decrees during the eighties.

This law governs the salaries and work conditions by activity sector. There are 22 decrees now operant, involving 16,000 employers and 140,000 employees, representing an important part of Quebec's work force. The large trade unions of Quebec believe this law to be very important because it represents a form of sectoral negotiation similar to the one that trade unions succeeded in imposing in the Quebec public sector. This law imposes salary standards to whole sectors of the economy such as the construction, clothing, furniture or window manufacturing industries. But this bizarre law strangles the job market and smothers the economy. The absurdity of this system is shown by the decree of 1992 imposing on building contractors an increase of 5% of salaries, even if the unemployment among construction employees is around 40%.

The Quebec Board of Trade has demonstrated the economic cost paid by these decrees. Clothing, furniture and wood transformation factories have experienced in Quebec a drop in employment of 15% during the eighties. In the meantime, in Ontario, employment in these sectors has actually increased by 36%.

There is a form of corporatism in this system, a surprising alliance between entrepreneur associations, government regulatory organizations and trade unions. This alliance aims at the elimination of competition and the maintenance of the old privileges at the expenses of the interests of those who want to work.

Let us take the case of Alain Jacques,[2] the owner of a cabinet-making company that had, in 1992, 60 employees. Inspectors from the Quebec Construction Board, helped by the Association of Construction Entrepreneurs of Quebec, fined him for paying wages inferior to the sectoral decree. Mr. Jacques then had to pay salaries at the same level as those of the building industry to his employees, who worked in a

2   Les Affaires, March 27, 1993.

small factory but also installed cabinets on the walls of his customers, thus "becoming" construction workers.

Today his 16 year-old company is in liquidation. Alain Jacques has decided to abandon his fight against foolish and merciless rules by becoming a simple craftsman.

Quebec, only a very small part of North America, still shows the reflexes of a bureaucratized society on the French model. We have to diminish the administrative load on the small and medium-size companies that are the economic hope of Quebec. Unless there is a sea change in this regulatory hodge-podge, inherited from another and very different era, Quebec's economy will continue to perform poorly.

CHAPTER SIX

Quebec Inc. and linguistic interventionism

THE QUIET REVOLUTION, symbol of Quebec's political and economic renewal, erupted in the sixties, and had as one of its consequences a wholesale rethinking and transformation of our system of education, health services and economics.

These tumultuous years brought us also a pronounced taste for State planning, as shown by the creation of numerous State corporations like the S.G.F., Sidbec and Soquem (in the mining and industrial sectors of the economy), and the S.D.I. and the Caisse de dépôt et placement in the financial sector. All of these corporations had as their goal the channeling of Quebecers' savings for the creation of jobs or to help Quebecers become independant of big Anglo-saxon capital. It was the tangible and logical conclusion of the well-known Liberal slogan "Masters in our own house". However, after several misadventures in heavy industry (Marine Industries) and in steel and iron ore (Sidbec-Dosco), it had become apparent that there was a chasm separating the planning of such industrial projects by well-intentioned but inexperienced technocrats, and the long-term profitability of such enterprises required to guarantee their survival and the maintenance of the jobs they created.

The success of the nationalisation of private hydro-electric companies under the leadership of Hydro-Québec in 1962 had engendered a certain amount of cockiness here in Quebec. It was easy to overlook, however, that managing a state monopoly was far easier than operating an industrial enterprise in a ferociously competitive international marketplace. And so, during those crazy years from 1962 to 1972, when it was still possible to borrow capital at 5.75% or 6% with the guaranty of the State, other industrial enterprises were set up, enterprises like Rexfor and Soquip (both of which turned out unhappily, especially if the criterion of investment returns using public funds is taken into account). Finally, in 1977, using as a pretext its electoral platform, the Quebec government made the enormous error of buying Asbestos Corporation, by then the symbol of an industry in decline. And it was done by paying the majority American shareholder handsomely, while offering nothing to local investors. A policy reversal occurred during the second mandate of the Parti Québécois however, and we also witnessed the introduction of privatization, a policy which continued after the election of Robert Bourassa's Liberal government in 1984.

At the end of 1966, I had just begun to work at the Caisse du dépôt et placement du Québec. It was clear to all the officers at the Caisse that those making policy in Quebec City had developed a firm belief in the advantages of state intervention. The use of the state as a collective tool was supposed to help francophones accede to positions of decision-making and also to create within Quebec a class of French Canadian leaders in business and industry, i.e. to be independant of Anglophone power. This latter group, at the beginning of the sixties, enjoyed an overwhelming predominance in the realm of the economy that many French Quebecers found inacceptable. This analysis led to a "made in Quebec" industrial policy by which, despite the sparse francophone competence in industry, a number of excellent candidates were recruited whose role was to put French Quebec solidly on the road to technological and industrial competency. Human resources were considered to be of utmost importance, even more rare and precious for the future of Quebec than capital which the government could easily borrow thanks to the low national debt left by the former régime of Maurice Duplessis.

CREATING THE WEALTH OF A NATION

The political leaders of Quebec, architects of the Quiet revolution, had quickly concluded that the creation of a modern educational system was the cornerstone of the rapid economic development which would enrich all Quebecers.

Originally a largely rural society, Quebec was thrown despite itself into the industrial revolution at the beginning of the twentieth century, overwhelmingly through foreign investment. Quebec's development was somewhat slowed by the Depression but accelerated again during World War II, and would, in the final analysis, continue to progress thanks to the competence and knowledge of all classes of society.

The State looked specifically at francophones to lead the enterprises newly created through its initiative. The hope was that the francophone presence at the top of a private sector still dominated by the English would also increase. The English, and by extension the numerous immigrants to Quebec who assimilated into anglophone culture as a result of Quebec's refusal to accept their children into French Catholic schools before 1963, already possessed the knowledge now sought for Francophones by the leaders of the State. As Francophones were subsequently able to do starting in 1963 under Jean Lesage, the English had put into place an efficient and competent modern school system and had fostered within their community the knowledge and traditions which supported their success in business and industry.

THE LINGUISTIC AND CONSTITUTIONAL DEBATES

The endless constitutional discussions and the debates on the nature of Quebec society that wore on from 1961 to 1976 created a climate of relative uncertainty among the English-speaking business class, and this class accounted for a large part of Quebec's economy up until the sixties. This uncertainty, combined with the fear of loss of privileges, led to the first waves of anglophone emigration out of Quebec. Some irate statements were aimed the way of René Lévesque in 1963 by the president of Noranda Mines, following Lévesque's having qualified the mentality of the privileged Westmount enclave as "Rhodesian". A neutral observer of this period would unfortunately have probably concluded that the monied classes of Westmount were in fact unable to find a *modus vivendi* with the francophone majority, but on the whole, most of Quebec's anglophone citizens were ready to seek some sort of compromise with the rising tide of Quebec nationalism. In point of fact, many traditionally unilingual anglophones discovered that learning the other language added something to their lives, and to their experience. Quite numerous were those who became proficient in French and were seriously interested in French Quebec culture.

After the 1976 electoral victory of the Parti québécois, the environment totally changed. Many anglophones had some initial sympathy with the "good government" electoral platform of the Parti québécois (a sizable part of the English vote went to this party as a protest against the Liberal Party's Bill 60, seen as too linguistically harsh). Initial enthusiasm turned to consternation, especially after the passage of Bill 101 in 1977. This law infuriated many anglophones even as it became a quasi religious symbol in French Québec, since the Parti Québécois won that election not for its separatist tendancies but on a platform of reform and efficiency in government. The new government initiated a series of measures intended to stimulate the economy, attract new investment and lower unemployment, which in Quebec was habitually higher than the Canadian average. These policy initiatives, made up of direct investment contributions from either the S.D.I or from the S.G.F. and the Caisse de dépôt, were, in conjunction with direct subsidies of all kinds, intended to create a stronger economic dynamic which would help Quebec catch up to Ontario.

The results of these enormous financial efforts were, for the Quebec taxpayers who shouldered their burden, not entirely successful. A large share of these new investments went into companies which did not survive the 1981-82 recession, or into large, often multinational corporations who had been attracted to Quebec by the low cost of electricity or by particularly generous federal and provincial industrial grants. But the most pernicious effect of these costly economic measures, which included the Quebec Stock Savings Plan and flow-through shares, was to push the marginal income tax rate in Quebec in 1978 to nearly 68%, nearly 10 per cent higher than Ontario's.

The right hand of government which sought to finance new investment by means of taxation, did not understand that the other hand of government was busy creating a situation that would, and here we are being charitable in our assessment, neutralize its efforts.

THE LANGUAGE LAWS

In 1972, the first Bourassa Liberal government had passed Bill 60, whose avowed aim was to promote the use of the French language in the day-to-day life of Quebec's citizens. This relatively moderate law was unable to satisfy Quebec nationalists who sensed that the power of the English minority was in a rout. After the 1976 electoral victory of the Parti Québécois, the now well-known Bill 101 was adopted in the National Assembly in 1977, without any consultation taking place with the various business groups who may have had some sober advice to give the lawmakers. Nor did these latter, and we must assume that it was with a certain satisfaction that they so acted, deign to consult with representatives of the Anglophone community which some in the PQ government saw as a privileged anachronism, an idle class living off the sweat of Quebec workers.

The consequences of the coming to power of the Parti Québécois and of the passage of Bill 101 were quickly to become apparent. Starting in 1976, the human capital constituted by Quebec's english-speaking citizens (who made up a large part part of the business and industrial class) began to emigrate to places where they were more welcome, Toronto, for instance, which received them and their skills with open arms. The anglophones had in fact two good reasons to leave : Bill 101 and the high level of income tax.

166

As for the francophone élite, it did all right for itself, sending its children to private schools where they learned enough English to respond to the requirements of the labour market. The majority of francophone Quebecers were somewhat less fortunate, as the unilingualism of the public school system to which most were confined limited their job possibilities.[1]

THE EXODUS

Montreal, a city which had justly taken pride in being the most important locus of head offices in Canada, now began to lose its centres of decision-making, one by one. Any concerned government would have gone to great lengths to staunch this economic bleeding, understanding that these head offices created and maintained high-level and well-remunerated managerial positions. As is well-known, the head office "industry" makes an important contribution to any country's, or in this case, city's development. Highly-paid jobs, the presence of decision-makers and their well-trained, knowledge-

---

[1] The bilingual reader is referred to the article by Professor Jean-Luc Migué of the National School of Public Administration(Laval University), published in Le Devoir on May 13, 1993. In this article, entitled "The growth of French through prosperity and free choice or its decline through linguistic protectionism" Migué makes an overwhelming demonstration of the folly of restrictive language laws.

able advisers, the power of technology and progress, are all a part of the social and economic richness represented by head offices, and they represent a unique power and more stable wealth than the kind of low-tech, often polluting factories that are quick to shut down and lay off workers during recessions.

In the face of this growing exodus however, the government of Quebec took a passive stance, a stance bordering on outright hostility. The attitude of a Party Québécois National Assembly member, a future Minister at that, is quite revealing in exemplifying the mentality of the times. In 1977, during a private conversation after Sun Life Insurance announced that its head office was moving to Toronto, this politician opined to me, "Let them go. In any case, we'll pass laws obliging companies operating on Quebec territory to have a head office in Quebec." When I objected that these new head offices would be only shells, regional sales offices with no real decision-making power, with all the important positions maintained in Toronto, he added that "Quebecers would have to adjust and in any case it would be a small price to pay on the road to independence".

This kind of semi-official attitude illustrated by the above comment resulted in the dilapidation of an important part of Quebec's non francophone human capital which went straight to the city of Toronto, which was already preparing in 1976 to surpass Montreal in many areas and claim for itself the title of Canada's metropolis.

TABLE XV
TENDANCIES OF ENGLISH-SPEAKING
QUEBECERS' MIGRATION, 1966-1986

	1966-71	1971-76	1976-81	1981-86	1966-86
From Quebec to the rest of Canada	99100	94100	131500	70600	395300
rom the rest of Canada to Quebec	46900	41900	25200	29000	143000
Net result	-52200	-52200	-106300	-41600	-252300
From other countries to Quebec	36900	32900	15400	12300	97500

Source : Termote (1991)

None of the possible measures that could have stopped the hemorrhage which accelerated following the Sun Life departure were taken: it was as if the government had, unconsciously perhaps, decided to let the English go. A number of "optimists" imagined with satisfaction the massive filling by francophone Quebecers of head office positions formerly occupied by anglophones. There was also the hope that local enterprises would step into the breach and take over the slack left by departing companies.

The reality, however, proved to be starkly different. It is true that numerous enterprises were created and also grew between 1976 and 1986. But this growth would have taken place anyway, despite the head office flight[2], and God only knows what the real growth of Quebec companies would have been without these departures. We did see the birth of a class of francophones who filled some of the positions created by new companies, and some Quebecers did in part replace the departed anglophones, but in jobs stemming from regional, not head offices. As a whole, the result of all this was quite mixed, and we will unfortunately never know, really, what the growth of Quebec and of its metropolis, Montreal might have been had the government chosen not to stifle the anglophone community in an attempt to preserve and protect the cultural patrimony of francophone quebecers.

2   Among the well-known companies that moved head offices to Toronto were the Bank of Montreal, Canron, Canadian Aviation Electronics(CAE), Canadian Industries Ltd (C.I.L.), Dupont and Royal Trust.

TABLE XVI

QUEBEC-ONTARIO COMPARISON OF POPULATION AND GROSS DOMESTIC PRODUCT

TRENDS FROM 1961-1976, 1976-1986 AND 1986-1991

Year	Population, Québec/Ontario %	GDP, Québec/Ontario %
1961	84,33	63,62
1976	75,44	61,00
1986	71,76	57,96
1991	68,38	56,70

Source : Statistics Canada

EPILOGUE

THE PERIOD OF EXPANSION that began in 1986 was unfortunately followed by a recession which has shown few signs of ending. This situation has, in Canada, gone hand in hand with constitutional discussions which also seem hopelessly endless. It is evident that the two together have created a climate of uncertainty which has slowed down job-creating investments.

Nothing whatever has yet been done to stem the apparently continuing anglophone exodus from Quebec, and the attempts made by the Bourassa government to improve Bill 101 through Bill178[1] only served to worsen the already gloomy views that Quebec's English-language citizens held of their fu-

---

1   In a speech in Ste-Adèle, Quebec on May 29, 1993, former Quebec superior court chief justice Jules Deschênes opined that Bourassa's use of the "Notwithstanding" clause in 1988 in order to impose Bill 178 resulted in five years of discord and the torpedoeing of the Meech Lake Constitutional Accord.

ture in the province. A recent study (Locher, 1992) found that 73.7 % of anglophone students (who have a remarkably high level of schooling) felt that within ten years' time they would no longer be living in Quebec.

I must conclude from the above that Quebec's economic decline relative to Ontario has coincided with the departure of anglophone Quebecers, especially during the years 1976 to 1986. Quebec undoubtedly became poorer with the loss of these people and the relocation of many Montreal head offices to Toronto. In fact, according to my estimates, Quebec has lost more than one billion dollars a year[2] in tax revenues because of the exodus of 150,000 anglophones during these years.

The government of Quebec confirms this hypothesis in a January 1993 document entitled *Living within our means*. According to this official publication, " The proportion of Canadian taxpayers with high revenues residing in Quebec, which was 23.9% in 1976, has since fallen sharply and stood at only 18.3% in 1985." This figure contrasts sharply

2   I estimate at $35,000 the average annual taxable income per departed Anglophone, or a total salary mass of $5.25 billion. Calculating an average 19% income tax rate applicable on Quebec's share of this revenue, and not counting the revenues generated by the provincial sales tax which would surely increase the loss, the figure of $1 billion plus is probably a conservative one.

with Quebec's 26% share of the total Canadian population for this latter year.

Some have tried to explain this phenomenon by positing a "natural" tendency for economic activity to move westward. Others have said that Anglophones left the province to seek work in more dynamic environments. But despite their well-known financial problems, neither Boston, nor New York for that matter, suffered the devastation which has befallen Montreal. The truth of the matter is that the anglophone exodus from Quebec followed the move of head offices out of the province, and because of a multiplier effect, this move towards Toronto had a net negative effect two to three times greater than the actual number of jobs directly lost.

In addition to this, Quebec government intervention in the economy through fiscal incentives (the Quebec Stock Savings Plan, flow-through shares) and through state investment in industry and in the Olympic installations, especially between the years 1972 and 1984, have contributed to a net relative impoverishment of the province. The real and fiscal losses engendered by many of these investments resulted in higher levels of taxation on Quebecers' income compared to those in Ontario, adding even more incentive on high wage-earners and their companies to leave Quebec. The sums thus lost also hindered our ability to invest in a better and more dynamic infrastructure without which no economy can prosper, and cut sharply into available funding for our public education system whose quality, or lack thereof, has a direct link to a successful and prosperous future for the province and its citizens.

In our economically interdependent world, in the context of the tripartite NAFTA accord for free trade recently signed by Canada, the United States and Mexico, it seems to me that it is still possible for Quebec to act by making a fundamental change in its language laws[3], in order to make them compatible with the Charter of Rights and Freedoms, and to modify its provincial and municipal tax levels to allow us to be more competitive, to become a more attractive place to transact business than we have recently been compared to our Canadian, American and Mexican neighbours.

3   The Bourassa government introduced Bill 86 while this book was in press. This new law, a quintessential and belated Bourassa compromise, relaxes somewhat the worst constraints of the language and sign laws and modifies the Charter of the French language.

TABLE XVII
COMPARATIVE INCOME TAX RATES
FOR AN INDIVIDUAL
(Maximum rates)

	QUEBEC	ONTARIO	U.S.A.[4]	MEXICO
1976	66,41	61,38	50,00	40,00
1977	63,07	61,92	50,00	40,00
1978	67,92	61,92	50,00	40,00
1979	67,92	61,92	50,00	40,00
1980	67,92	61,92	50,00	40,00
1981	67,92	62,78	50,00	40,00
1982	60,40	50,32	50,00	40,00
1983	60,40	50,32	50,00	40,00
1984	60,40	50,32	50,00	40,00
1985	62,40	52,02	50,00	40,00
1986	59,50	55,42	50,00	40,00
1987	56,60	52,53	38,50	40,00
1988	51,10	46,11	33,00	40,00
1989	49,80	47,15	33,00	40,00
1990	50,50	48,23	33,00	35,00
1991	51,10	49,10	31,00	35,00
1992	51,00	49,80	31,00	35,00

Source : Price Financial Services Inc.

4   Certain American and Mexican States also have a personal income tax which can amount to approximately 6% of taxable income.

ABOUT THE AUTHOR

Pierre Arbour was born in Shawinigan, Quebec in 1935. After obtaining a B.A. from the University of Montreal in 1956 and a B.Com from McGill in 1959, he pursued a career in the financial world. In 1962 he became a sales representative and analyst for a Montreal stockbroker. In 1966, he was named the first head of the variable income portfolio at the *Caisse de dépôt et placement du Québec.*

In early 1976 he was promoted to the newly-created post of Senior Corporate Investment Advisor and was a member of the Caisse's Investment Committee. In his new role, Pierre Arbour was involved in financial restructuring, as board representative for the Caisse de dépôt, in the following public and para-public companies : Gaz Métropolitain, Horne and Pitfield (Edmonton), M. Loeb (Ottawa), National Drug and Chemicals (Montréal), Place Desjardins (Montreal), Provigo(Montreal) and the Société de développement industriel du Québec (S.D.I.).

In April 1979, he left the Caisse de dépôt to create Alkebec Inc., a venture capital firm which he still presides. From 1979 to 1990 he was also president of a publicly-owned oil and gas exploration company.

In 1980, he became a director of Consolidated-Bathurst Inc. until its sale in 1989 to Stone Container of Chicago.

Mr. Arbour is also a director of several other public and private companies and is a vice-president of Mexperts Inc., a consulting firm specializing in mexican investments.

179

Lithographié au Canada
sur les presses de
Métrolitho – Sherbrooke